# POST BASIC

## THE THEATRE NURSE AND THE LAW

# The Theatre Nurse and the Law

## Eileen Dixon

CROOM HELM
London & Sydney

©1984 Eileen Dixon
Croom Helm Ltd, Provident House, Burrell Row,
Beckenham, Kent BR3 1AT
Croom Helm Australia Pty Ltd, First Floor,
139 King Street, Sydney, NSW 2001, Australia

British Library Cataloguing in Publication Data

Dixon, Eileen P.
    The theatre nurse and the law.
    1. Operating room nursing—Law and legislation—England
    I. Title
    344.204'414      KD2968.N8

ISBN 0-7099-0818-0

Printed and bound in Great Britain
by Billing & Sons Limited, Worcester.

# CONTENTS

Preface     vii

1. Individual and Patient Rights     9

2. Litigation and the Extended Role of the Nurse     16

3. Consent     22

4. Objections to Surgery     30

5. Lack of Communication     49

6. The Nurse's Liability for Negligence     56

7. Accidents to Patients and Staff     63

8. Record-keeping     73

9. Terminal Illness and Issues of the Dying Patient     83

10. Organ Transplantation     94

11. The Coroner's Court     109

12. International Legal Positions on Surgery     124

Table of Statutes and Statutory Instruments Used for Reference     137

Index     138

# PREFACE

Ignorantia juris neminem excusat. (Ignorance of the law excuses no one.)

This principle of English law derives from the system of civil law which evolved in the Roman state from the time of Justinian and this Roman law is still the basis of a large part of European jurisprudence.

Our daily life is governed to a great extent by the belief that those around us will do their duty and this belief relies wholly on trust. However, no profession whose functions are as diverse as nursing can hope to survive solely on trust and greater emphasis needs to be placed on a systematic development of the teaching of the Law in relation to professional practice.

History has shown that mankind meets its problems first by learning from its experience, but as the problems increase so a strategy is developed to deal with them. Experience can be an effective teacher, but for the professional nurse, caring for the surgical patient necessitates a sound knowledge which covers not only the performance of skills but also the legal responsibilities of the work. In the past, clinically orientated nurses have tended to look to others for guidance and legal protection but the development of professional nursing together with the power and freedom of patients to resort to litigation only serves to emphasise the urgent need for a change in direction of nurse education.

Alarming statistics give cause for concern over the increasing awards being made by the courts in negligence cases. However, Harry Greene, late Professor of Pathology at Yale, has said: 'statistics are like a bikini – what they reveal is extremely interesting; but what they conceal is infinitely more intriguing'. The nurse in the operating theatre should be sufficiently knowledgeable and confident to resist changes that would threaten the quality of care or usurp professional and personal liberties for herself and her patients. Defensive medicine benefits no one, least of all the patient, and the theatre nurse, as an important member of the team, must be able to practise her art in the sure knowledge that her contribution to the patient's wellbeing is an integral part of his treatment. The introduction of the Nursing Process has helped to turn the spotlight on the important role the theatre nurse has to play, as it identifies elements in the care of patients which do not come into the orbit of medicine or any other discipline.

This book is written primarily for nurses working in theatre but it is hoped that it will be useful to all staff involved in the care of surgical patients. It has been my endeavour to provide information which will help the nurse to practise within the law, while continuing to provide the compassionate care which must continue to remain the hallmark of her profession. The text is equally applicable to male and female members of the profession.

## Acknowledgements

My sincere thanks are due to the many people who helped in the production of this book, in particular Mrs H. Robertson, Librarian in the School of Nursing, Guy's Hospital, for her unfailing help; Helen Thomas, Assistant Librarian at the Royal College of Nursing; and my daughter, Anne Marie, for her help and encouragement.

# 1 INDIVIDUAL AND PATIENT RIGHTS

The Law can be defined as the totality of rules emanating from various sources actually realised and enforceable in any organised state. It is something that changes and can be altered if justice demands it. English Law is partly written and partly unwritten. Written Law is Statute Law and it consists of Acts of Parliament; a good deal of English Law rests on custom, or what has been done before, and is called case Law.

Liberty is the very breath of existence and it allows the individual to live a life of personal independence. The Law protects this freedom but it also governs the actions of society. Every law must have a sanction and this sanction must consist of some punishment inflicted upon the law-breaker.

In the past, the nurse in the operating theatre concerned herself mainly with perfecting skills, whilst the legal aspects of surgery were considered the responsibility of the surgeon. This situation is now rapidly changing and the nurse can no longer hide behind her traditional role (see Chapter 2). Nursing has been in a constant state of change for the past 20 years and nowhere has this been more apparent than in the operating theatre. The twentieth-century theatre nurse must be a competent professional who can be judged according to the way she exercises her discretion and professional judgement in a particular situation. She is, and must be held to be, responsible for her own actions and nothing can totally absolve her of this responsibility.

The watchword of the International Council of Nurses for the next quadrennium is 'Freedom', and worldwide, we see daily evidence of people reaffirming their right to freedom. While prostitutes in London are asserting their right to ply their trade there are many people in Third World countries begging for the right to have enough food to keep body and soul together.

A 'right' can be defined as a just claim, but what is considered just will be determined by the laws and culture of a particular country. In the Middle Ages, an assertion of personal freedom would have been considered a crime and even now, in the twentieth century, what we are told is legally right may seem morally and ethically wrong. Total freedom does not eixst; from Queen to commoner, we must all render obedience to the Law, and therefore the rights of the individual can only be considered within this framework. Individual rights are well protected by the Law. Religious and political freedom are taken for granted and, provided we do not harm other people, we can do much as we like.

On the face of it, it seems quite reasonable to say that we all have the right to life, but of course this is not true. On the one hand the fight for abortion on demand continues while on the other pressure groups are campaigning for the legalisation of euthanasia. The progress made in surgical procedures in this century continues to pose moral, legal and ethical problems for theatre nurses, and for some of these problems at least, there is no quick and easy answer. The voice of conscience will often be in conflict with what we are told is right and proper but the dictates of reason, a sense of justice and common sense should help to solve some of the dilemmas.

Surgical nurses, in one form or another, have been with us for a long time; lack of anatomical knowledge did not deter surgeons from earliest times from performing operations, and then as now there was a need for 'good' women to care for the patients, despite Charles Dickens' opinion of nurses of his time who were depicted as gin-swigging Sairey Gamp and Betsy Prig. However, it was only in 1919 that the nursing profession gained statutory recognition, although in Scotland there was a Register of Nurses in the Scottish Poor Law service from 1885 to 1919, and in the ensuing years the General Nursing Council has fought long and hard to improve standards and conditions for nurses.

Society has changed considerably over the years and much credit for improving working conditions must go to the unions; no longer can children be forced to work down the mines or clean chimneys. The working week gets shorter all the time and there is now adequate machinery to seek redress if a wrong is thought to be done – for example, though acts and organisations such as the Employment Protection Act 1975, the Sex Discrimination Act, the Equal Pay Act 1970, the professional bodies and the unions.

Some people might say that we live in a law-ridden society. In August 1982 a Law lecturer was summoned under a 138-year-old by-law for playing football in the street. By doing some research into the 69 by-laws passed by his city's leaders in 1844, he uncovered a huge catalogue of crimes that can be committed in everyday living. Did you know that it's an offence for anyone in Sheffield to clean his windows while standing on a sill, unless he lives in a basement? Burning an effigy is also against the law – so be careful on Guy Fawkes night![1] Nevertheless, we need laws to protect our rights. We are kept well informed that all types of crime are on the increase and now, more than ever, we need the protection of the Law in the form of the police. Fortunately for us in the UK, they do not resort to industrial action.

The theatre nurse is protected by her professional qualification, but she is also responsible for her professional behaviour, first to the General Nursing Council and secondly to her employing authority. If she honours these responsibilities she will give safe patient care and she has nothing to fear from the Law. Patients also have rights as citizens and these rights still exist when they are in hospital. The Metropolitan Poor Law Act of 1867 upheld the philosophy that pauper patients must be less comfortable than the lowest paid worker.[2] But no longer do patients have to be grateful for charity, as in the days of the Poor Law:

The National Health Service Act 1977, in referring to the duty of the Secretary of State, states he will

(1) continue the promotion in England and Wales of a comprehensive health service designed to secure improvement
(a) in the physical and mental health of the people of those countries, and
(b) in the prevention, diagnosis and treatment of illness, and for that purpose to provide or secure the effective provision of services in accordance with this Act.
(2) The services so provided shall be free of charge except in so far as the making and recovery of charges is expressly provided for by or under any enactment, whenever passed.

In part III of the Act, under the heading 'Additional powers as to services and supplies; and the use of those services and supplies for private patients', it states

58. The Secretary of State may allow persons to make use (on such terms, including terms as to the payment of charges, as he thinks fit) of any accommodation or services provided

under this Act and may provide the accommodation or services in question to an extent greater than that necessary apart from this section if he thinks it expedient so to do in order to allow persons to make use of them. This section is subject to sections 59, 60 and 62.

Section 59 (2) states

The Secretary of State shall not in the exercise of his section 58 power afford a person admission or access to accommodation or services at such a hospital as a private patient unless satisfied that the accommodation or services are required for the purposes of investigation, diagnosis or treatment which –
(a) is of a specialised nature or involves the use of specialised equipment or skills; and
(b) is not privately available in Great Britain or, if it is so available either –
(I) is not privately available there at a place which is reasonably accessible to the patient; or
(II) is such that it is in the interest of the health service or of the Scottish health service or of both for it to be carried out on that occasion at that hospital.
In this subsection 'privately available' means available at a satisfactory standard otherwise than at a health service hospital.

I have deliberately quoted this rather 'wordy' extract from the Act in the hope that it will help to clarify some of the confusion which exists for theatre nurses regarding the rights of National Health patients versus private patients.

The Trade Union and Labour Relations Act 1974 repealed the whole of the Industrial Relations Act 1971. A provision of the Act which is substantially unchanged is that peaceful picketing is permitted; however, it must not involve obstruction of the highway. There are also restrictions on the number of pickets and on secondary and tertiary picketing.

When 20-year-old Mrs Laura Purkiss collapsed in premature labour the ambulance rushed her to St. Bartholomew's Hospital, London, only to be turned away at the hospital gates by a NUPE strike picket. There was a delay of over an hour before Mrs Purkiss was smuggled into the hospital by a goods entrance. Too late. Her unborn baby died.[3]

Many of the decisions we make in our everyday life are quite ordinary – what to wear, where to go, what to eat. Other decisions are not ordinary at all, but the moral choice is so obvious that we react with rapid action. When we are faced with making a decision to which the Law has given its blessing and is condoned by society, yet we believe it to be ethically and morally wrong, then only conscience can decide.

Considerable journalistic coverage has been given to the now famous Rule 12, for members of the Royal College of Nursing. This rule states

Neither the Council nor any Officer or Official of the College nor any membership Entity of the College shall be empowered to initiate or be a party to the withdrawal of service of Members of the College in furtherance of an industrial dispute unless or until the policy of the College in respect of industrial action by nurses is changed by College in General Meeting. A Resolution passed by a two thirds majority shall be required to change such established policy and provision shall be made for proxy voting thereon. Alternatively, the College in General Meeting may empower the Council to take a decision in respect of limited industrial action if circumstances should be such as to warrant such action. Again, a two thirds majority of the members present or voting by proxy at a General Meeting shall be required so to authorise the Council.

The General Nursing Council for England and Wales made a pronouncement on whether a nurse who limits or withdraws his or her services could face proceedings for professional misconduct, and it reads as follows:

The Council is of the opinion that if a nurse puts the health, safety or welfare of his or her patients at risk by taking strike or other industrial action he or she would have a case to answer on the score of professional misconduct, just as he or she would if the health, safety or welfare of patients were put at risk by any other action on his or her part.[4]

This document explains this statement in further detail and is essential reading for all nurses.

The Mental Health (Amendment) Act came into force in September 1983. It deals with the right of detained mentally ill and handicapped patients. Consent to treatment is a controversial issue of the Act; leucotomy may not now be performed without a second opinion and non-consenting patients are given ECT only with the approval of a Mental Health Act Commissioner.

Different societies reach different conclusions as to what is right and wrong. Nevertheless, however much the Law or society approve, individuals will ultimately base their decisions on their own values. Nurses have responsibilities both as individuals and professionals and their decisions must always be in accordance with the Law.

Legal history was made in May 1978 when a husband lost his fight to prevent his wife having an abortion. Mr Patton said he had the right of a say in the destiny of the child he had conceived but Sir George Baker, President of the Family Division of the High Court, told him that his application was 'completely misconceived'.[5]

A world 'first' in genetic engineering gave a childless woman the right to produce the first test-tube baby, gaining for her and her doctor an alleged sum of £325,000 for the newspaper and magazine rights for the story.[6]

Under the terms of the Abortion Act 1967, termination of pregnancy may be carried out by a medical practitioner subject to the conditions of the Act. Nurses have the right to refuse to participate in this procedure but with the following proviso:

(2) nothing in subsection (1) of this section shall affect any duty to participate in treatment which is necessary to save the life or to prevent grave permanent injury to the physical or mental health of a pregnant woman.[7]

**Summary**

Man can never be free; every individual must submit himself to the ordinances of the community. Within each man is conscience and it is to conscience that we must ultimately look when the views and thinking of society conflict with our own. Dissent may mean making a public disagreement but if the cause is just our democratic system of Law gives us the freedom to challenge.

The Law does not exist in the abstract; in the United Kingdom, we are allowed to persuade a majority of the nation to enact laws, which we ourselves wish to govern national life. As nurses, we must respect the rights of our patients, respecting their right of choice. Our professional qualification is not unrestricted and we must be guided in our professional behaviour by constitutionally–made laws, professional standards and our moral obligation to ensure that we 'do the sick no harm'.

## References

1. 'The Law is an old ass', *Daily Star*, 19 August 1982.
2. Monica Baly, *Nursing*, B.T. Batsford, 1977.
3. 'Nasty', *Sunday Express*, 14 March 1982.
4. Article by the Registrar, General Nursing Council for England and Wales, in *Nursing Mirror*, 4 October 1979.
5. 'Abortion go-ahead', *Evening Standard*, 24 May 1978.
6. '£325,000 for first test-tube baby', *Evening Standard*, 11 July 1978.
7. Abortion Act 1967.

# 2 LITIGATION AND THE EXTENDED ROLE OF THE NURSE

Many theatre nurses believe that they are being asked to perform duties which are outside the scope of their nursing practice. For some, at least, this is a challenge which they are quite happy to accept but for others it can be a nightmare: junior nurses left on their own to 'scrub' for cases they know little or nothing about; a new sister who is expected to manage a theatre without prior induction; Joint Board students who, because they are trained nurses, are magically expected to become theatre nurses over night.

Shortage of staff and the need to 'get through the lists' are the most common excuses for this appalling state of affairs. Would you believe that during the Crimean War, Florence Nightingale refused to allow her nurses to lift a finger to help, without the express and prior approval of the doctors? Yet here are nurses in the 1980s prepared to be 'mini-surgeons', often without the permission of their employing authority and without any legal cover, while non-nursing staff are allowed to perform the very functions for which nurses are trained, i.e. caring for patients.

Long before litigation became an everday word in the language of theatre nurses, surgeons were quite happy to have the theatre sister assist him during surgery: retracting, cutting sutures and even suturing. Junior surgeons were grateful for her help and tactful advice; she had seen it all before and like the ward sister of old, she had the authority to set her own high standards which everyone was expected to maintain. It is difficult to pinpoint an exact time at which this situation changed. Some people blame the Salmon Report for taking authority away from the sister by creating the role of Nursing Officer; perhaps it was due to the introduction of formal job descriptions which made everyone look at the many tasks which made up their day's work. Or is it due to a new breed of emancipated nurses who dare to question ritual, or has society become more demanding? Whatever the reason, it is now a fact of nursing life that no nurse in theatre should perform any task for which she has not been trained and is not legally covered. Reflecting on this, it sounds good common sense, but it is very difficult for some people to change the habits of a lifetime.

Medical litigation is becoming more common. As yet, the occasions when the theatre nurse's negligence becomes a public issue are rare, but it is inevitable that this situation will change.

'As a result of anaesthetic accidents at the Kent & Canterbury Hospital in March (1977) two patients die. Another patient at the Westminster Hospital suffered permanent brain damage as the result of an almost identical set of circumstances.' Mary Donn was a member of the Westminster Committee of Enquiry and in an interview with *Nursing Times* she said 'I think that we must, as a matter of urgency, look closely at our acceptance of responsibility . . . I think that often we accept responsibility without realising what we are doing and without questioning it.'[1]

'Untrained nurses in anaesthetic accident'; thus read a headline in the *Nursing Mirror* of September 1977. The article described a system at Victoria Hospital, Worksop, which allowed untrained nurses to take charge of post-operative recovery patients. This system came in for severe criticism from an enquiry team investigating an incident where an 18-month-old boy failed to recover consciousness after a right inguinal hernia operation and is now a severe spastic. It seems that a number of unfortunate circumstances led to this tragic accident. In its report, the enquiry, stressed that an unconscious patient should only be handed over to a fully qualified nurse for recovery, and should not be passed to an unqualified nurse until he has regained consciousness. The report further states that 'if current staffing makes this an impractical plan, an additional post should be created for a nurse to work in theatre during operating sessions and on the ward at other times'.

The immediate reaction of theatre nurses on reading this is likely to be one of horror. How could anyone allow a little child to suffer needlessly because of negligence? Didn't anyone care? But before anyone can criticise, it would be wise to look at the reality in many theatres where, but for the grace of God, the very same tragedy could occur. Theatre nurses are really not becoming more careless, just more visible. The powerful pressure to accept the *status quo* has presented many problems in theatre: no one likes to be unpopular; we continually talk about teamwork and it takes great courage for any theatre nurse to draw the attention of her superiors to a practice which she considers dangerous, particularly if it is well-established.

Nursing has been called a vocation, a calling, even an occupation, but it is generally accepted as a profession. However, when we compare it with other professions we see that whereas lawyers or teachers practise within their particular profession, nurses are generally part of a multidisciplinary team. Midwives are probably the only exception as their qualification allows them to practise alone. Total independence is impossible for the theatre nurse; she can never be totally emancipated from the control of the surgeon because of the traditional relationship between doctors and nurses, but more realistically, because it is at the invitation of the surgeon that the patient is in theatre. Quite simply, the nurse's role is to supply the equipment for the operation and she is reponsible for and answerable to the patient and his family for her nursing of him. However, the concept of teamwork is strong in theatre staff and they see this as doing whatever has to be done. Therefore they are more than willing to assist the surgeon if the houseman or registrar is absent. They will apply diathermy, apply and remove haemostats, retract and even suture. This is all very well, but what is the position of the theatre nurse if something goes wrong?

She will have to accept that she is functioning in an extended role when performing these tasks and although in most cases the surgeon will agree that she was acting under his instruction, it could well be said that if nursing staff have time to act as surgeons' assistants the theatre is either overstaffed or the nurses are neglecting their nursing duties. Nurses in the intensive care unit may also find themselves in a similar position: they may be expected to change tracheostomy tubes, extubate, defibrillate, and discontinue and recommence ventilation in patients who are being weaned off.

While it is true that in the USA nurses are trained in anaesthesia and are legally covered to administer general anaesthetics, that is not the case in Britain. The nurse working in the anaesthetic room may find herself preparing intravenous drugs and, in certain circumstances, she may even be left in total charge of the anaesthetised patient. Again, many nurses are quite capable of carrying out these tasks, but there must be a hospital policy which clearly states that the employing authority is in agreement that nurses function in this extended role and the policy should further state that the employing authority is prepared to accept responsibility for the nurse.

Many of the tasks mentioned have been seen as nursing duties through 'custom and practice', but if, as the result of an unqualified person carrying out a medical task, a patient is injured or dies, it is most likely that in any ensuing legal action the doctrine of 'res ipsa loquitor'[2] will apply.

The well-publicised case of Mrs Carol Brown should act as a warning for any nurse unsure of what she is doing.

A report by the Area Health Authority and the South West Thames Regional Health Authority has been presented before the public, in which officers finally accept that they were in the wrong and that the legal advice they were given was equally wrong . . . the nursing inquiry had found breaches of procedure by both midwives in the topping up of the epidural injection initially made by a doctor. Neither of the midwives held the necessary certificate of competence, and the sister in charge had been reprimanded.[3]

Mrs Brown was awarded record damages of £414,563. A 38-year-old old former model, she is now unable to move apart from partial use of her right hand and arm. How many nurses, in theatre, intensive care or the surgical wards, have actually completed a course which allows them to carry out this procedure or give intravenous injections? Not only must they have a certificate of competence, but the certificate must be one awarded by their employing authority. It is not sufficient that they obtained one from a different employing authority during previous employment.

There are no automatic answers for the theatre nurse faced with the dilemma of functioning in an extended role. Each situation must be looked at separately, discussed with the theatre manager and the legal position of the nurse clarified by the employing authority. If a decision is made that the nurse is allowed to perform certain extra duties, she will have to provide evidence of competence.

We should not allow doctors to dictate nursing care. They are rightly responsible for the patient's medical treatment; they investigate, diagnose and then prescribe the most appropriate treatment for the patient. They are also legally responsible for decisions about admission and discharge of patients and their treatment. The theatre nurse is not trained to perform surgery, administer anaesthesia or prescribe drugs – she is qualified to nurse and is skilled in theatre technique. Would it not be wiser to encourage her to extend her role within the confines of her profession rather than attempt to encroach on a very well established profession which is already over-subscribed? It is important that doctors and nurses work together if the patient is to have the best possible treatment. Each brings to the patient his or her own particular skills and expertise. The more the theatre nurse is encouraged to allow herself to be used as a dumping ground for jobs for the convenience of other professionals, the more she is likely to become a 'jack of all trades but master of none'.

Many accidents to patients are attributed to shortage of nursing staff, particularly staff with a specialised training such as renal, intensive care or theatre. If these highly skilled people are to perform medical tasks, who will actually nurse the patients? The Lewin Report[4] introduced the grade of Operating Department Assistant in theatre to 'complement the work of the nursing staff'. We already have nurse's aides and nursing auxillaries. Will another report recommend the introduction of another grade to 'complement the work of the ODAs', who by then will have had to take over the work of the nursing staff who are kept busy in their extended role? It could happen.

**Summary**

There will always be room for new ideas in nursing and nurses must be prepared to move with the times if they are to survive. Never before have we as theatre nurses faced such a challenge: much more to learn, new equipment and techniques, an increase in the number and grades of ancillary staff and continual reminders that we must be accountable for everything we do. Perhaps it is understandable that in this climate there are some nurses who are prepared to carry out almost any task in theatre if only to justify their presence. Nevertheless, when a nurse holds a qualification which allows her to practise particular skills, she must not assume that this qualification also entitles her to perform the duties of her medical colleagues.

She is not practising on her own and should remember that she is part of a team, each member having his or her own responsibilities. She must at all costs resist the temptation to take on duties for which she has not been trained and is not legally covered. If she does, and the patient subsequently suffers damage, litigation can result because there has been a breach of a duty of care owed by the nurse to the patient.

Doctors too, owe this duty of care and if a doctor unreasonably instructs a nurse to perform any task which is recognised as his duty then the nurse has the right to refuse, that is unless there is an agreed hospital policy that nurses are legally covered to perform doctor's duties and the nurse has a contract to this effect. Physicians' assistants already exist in the United States, so we must decide now whether or not we too need this grade of staff in Britain.

Theatre nursing is now under the professional microscope and some people are asking if we really need nurses in theatre. If there is evidence to suggest that we do then let's not try to be mini-doctors, but use our expertise to give *nursing* care.

## References and Note

1. Mary Donn, *Nursing Times*, Theatre Nursing supplement, 6 October 1977.
2. 'Res ipsa loquitor' – the thing speaks for itself.
3. Mike McCormack, 'AHA's attitude was "scandalous" ', *Nursing Mirror*, 10 March 1982.
4. The Lewin Report, HMSO, 1968.

# 3 CONSENT

Considerable confusion continues to exist among nurses regarding consent to surgery: when is it necessary?, what is meant by informed consent?, is obtaining the patient's consent to surgery a nursing responsibility?, should consent always be written?. These are just some of the questions asked by nurses.

Let us start by defining 'consent' as an agreement by a patient to submit to treatment which has been explained to him by the doctor. It therefore follows that treating a patient, without his consent, is an unauthorised interference with his body for which the surgeon, theatre staff and, ultimately, the Health Authority may be held responsible.

In the complex technological society in which modern medicine exists there is continual pressure on nurses to be well informed. Shortage of staff can increase the demands on theatre staff and there is an ever-present danger that consent can be regarded as no more than a routine ritual. However, with some exceptions, patients are free to refuse any form of treatment proposed. In a society that values freedom and justice the individual is permitted the right to choose and, as far as possible, this must be respected. Another very real consideration is the fact that the public is now more ready to seek redress of a wrong through the courts.

When a patient decides to submit to surgery this decision will inevitably be based on values. Values represent a way of life and give it direction. They may be based on a belief in good conduct and moral behaviour, the precepts of God as revealed to man, tradition, culture or custom. The decision will be further based on the information given to the patient by the surgeon. It is interesting to note that in Britain there is no legal obligation on the surgeon to give a detailed explanation of the proposed operation; it is sufficient that a clear but non-technical explanation is given, although all questions asked by the patient must be accurately answered. Now, bearing in mind that many patients are worried by the very thought of having an operation, some are of limited intelligence and the doctor-patient relationship is often based on the belief that the doctor is too busy to answer

22

questions, the nurse who is caring for the patient should ensure that any concern or uncertainty expressed by him regarding the operation should be conveyed to the surgeon. It is not a nursing responsibility to inform the patient or to get his consent; this is solely the surgeon's responsibility. Communication between medical and nursing staff regarding the patient's treatment is essential, and if more attention was paid to this, nurses would be spared the embarrassment of having to avoid some patients' questions because of ignorance of what he has been told. All members of the team, in the ward or theatre, must share information in order that there is continuity of care.

*Speller's Law Relating to Hospitals and Kindred Institutions*[1] cites a number of cases which gives support to the belief that 'he [the patient] must have been given – 'even without his having asked – such reasonable explanation of the nature and effect of what is proposed to be done as is appropriate and practicable in the circumstances, taking into account such things as the patient's level of understanding and his physical condition'. Findings in the cases cited show that should a patient bring an action claiming damages, alleging that the surgeon was negligent in answering questions, the plaintiff (patient) has to show evidence that his questions were not answered frankly and that his injuries resulted from this. We have now established that for consent to be valid, it must be *informed*.

**Who Can Give Informed Consent?**

A rational patient, of full age, who is not under the influence of drink or drugs.

**Who Cannot Give Informed Consent?**

(1) Unconscious patients.
(2) Mentally disordered patients. The Mental Health Act 1959 did not specifically state who should give consent for surgery on behalf of a mentally disordered patient, although it was generally accepted that the decision to operate should be made by the responsible medical officer or, in certain circumstances, by a close relative. The Mental Health

23

(Amendment) Act 1982 now stipulates that for informal patients, consent and a second opinion is required for 'any surgical operation for destroying brain tissue or for destroying the functioning of brain tissue' and for 'such other forms of treatment as may be specified for the purposes of this section by regulations made by the Secretary of State'. (Part VI, 43(1) Consent to treatment)

(3) Children.

## Consent to Examination is Not Required in the Following Circumstances[2]

On admission to Her Majesty's prison;
on a Court order, of a person suffering from a notifiable disease or tuberculosis;
on the probation order of a Court;
of immigrants at ports or airports;
of milk or food handlers;
of schoolchildren in state schools.

## Age of Consent

In the UK, a person becomes legally of age at 18 years and when the death penalty was in force this was the earliest age at which it could be applied. At majority, full legal rights and obligations are assumed: the right to vote, responsibility for one's own actions and debts and the responsibility to either volunteer or be conscripted in war. The term 'minor' is used to denote a person under 18 years, but it may also be used when referring to someone between 16 and 18 years:

The consent of a minor who has attained the age of 16 years to any surgical, medical or dental treatment which, in the absence of consent, would constitute a trespass to his person, shall be as effective as it would be if he were of full age; and where a minor has by virtue of this section given an effective consent to any treatment it shall not be necessary to obtain any consent for it from his parent or guardian. (S 8 Family Law Reform Act 1969)

## Consent for Those Aged 0 to 16 Years

There is no hard and fast rule as to the exact age at which a child can be said to have reached the age of reason, but 7 years seems to be the accepted age. This is of course assuming that the child is mentally normal and of average intelligence for his age. In the case of a minor – 7 to 16 years – coming to casualty for treatment, his submission to subsequent treatment implies his consent. Much, of course, will depend on exactly how much and what type of treatment is required. Cleaning and dressing of an abrasion or bandaging of a sprain can safely be carried out without consent of a parent or guardian but should more extensive treatment – e.g. surgery, however minor, with or without an anaesthetic – be required, then if time allows the consent of parent or guardian must be obtained.

## Types of Consent

### Implied Consent

As in the case of a child attending at casualty for treatment, the same principle applies with adults. In view of the increased importance of accurate record-keeping it would be most unwise to rely on implied consent for any surgical procedure, however minor.

### Oral Consent

It is the practice in National Health hospitals that patients are normally first seen by the hospital doctor in an outpatients clinic. Should it be decided that further tests, e.g. cystoscopy or aortography, are necessary in order to make an accurate diagnosis, the doctor will explain the procedure to the patient. Should surgery be considered the treatment of choice, this too will be explained and the patient can then decide whether or not to accept the treatment. He may then agree, orally, and subsequently arrive in the hospital on the appointed day for admission. If at no time he objects to the subsequent treatment, oral consent is legally acceptable. 'Silence gives consent'.

### Written Consent

This is the safest and most powerful evidence of consent,

provided it is informed. The surgeon explains the procedure to the patient, answering accurately any questions asked. The patient is then asked to read the consent form and when he indicates that he understands it, he is requested by the surgeon to sign it. To be valid, this must be done before any premedication is given and from an ethical and humane viewpoint, it should be completed the day before surgery, if possible. It cannot be overemphasised that a patient's signature, in itself, is not absolute evidence of consent. Only when all the conditions are met, can the completed form be considered valid.

In the past, a multiplicity of forms have been used to record consent, and this has caused confusion, particularly for nurses moving from one hospital to another. While it is true that nurses in National Health hospitals will not be directly involved in obtaining a patient's consent for surgery, it is essential that they are aware of the correct procedure. It is not enough that they blindly follow orders and regulations through habit and un-questionably accept them. Education and training are the lifeblood of any profession and nurses involved in the care of surgical patients must acquire a general factual awareness of the current status of the Law governing their responsibilities and duties, and its application to their particular sphere of work. Only then can they recognise the responsibilities and limitations of their professional conduct.

The Department of Health and Social Security sent a circular to National Health Service hospital authorities on 2 February 1971 regarding consent forms. In essence, this document stated that after discussion with the British Medical Association, the Medical Defence Union, the Medical Protection Society and the Medical and Dental Defence Union of Scotland, agreement had been reached on a standard consent form to be used 'in the generality of medical and dental procedures for which consent is required'. Within this agreement is the statement 'no objection to the use of special consent forms for particular purposes (e.g. in connection with primary sterilisation procedures) . . .'. A recom-mended consent form is shown on the following page.

Any deletions, insertions or amendments to the form are to be made before the explanation is given and the form submitted for signature. If this form is used correctly, it will be a permanent record which will remain with the patient's notes. It will help to avoid misunderstandings and it may even help to avoid legal

---

I .............................. of .............................. Hospital
.............................. of .............................. hereby
consent to* the submission of my child
                                 ward
.............................. to undergo the operation
of .............................. the nature and purpose
of which have been explained to me by Dr/Mr* .........
I also consent to such further or alternative operative
measures as may be found necessary during the
course of the above-mentioned operation and to the
administration of general, local or other anaesthetics
for any of these purposes.
No assurance has been given to me that the operation
will be performed by any particular practitioner.
Date .............................. Signed ..............................
                         (patient/parent/guardian)*
I confirm that I have explained the nature and purpose
of this operation to the patient/parent/guardian.*
Date .............................. Signed ..............................
                         (medical/dental practitioner)
*Delete as appropriate

---

proceedings at a later date; but more important it is evidence that
the patient has been treated as a human being with the right to
make a choice.

In the USA, the principle of consent permits an informed
patient to limit the authorisation to specific bounds, and accept
the consequences of the surgeon not proceeding further.[4] Of
course the surgeon can choose not to enter a doctor/patient
relationship.

On the recommended consent form, the statement that no
assurance has been given that any particular surgeon will perform
the operation, affords very necessary protection for the surgeon.
I recall a situation which occurred many years ago when, if this
statement had been included on the consent form, a large amount
of money would have been saved.

An attractive young woman presented herself at the consulting rooms of a plastic surgeon, imploring his help. She had a problem which was socially embarrassing and psychologically disturbing – pendulous breasts. The surgeon agreed to perform a mammoplasty and she was duly admitted and had her operation. She had a slight wound infection post-operatively and discussed this with a young doctor who examined her wound. She questioned whether this infection might have occurred during the operation, but he assured her that he had performed the operation, as his boss was on leave, and everything had gone very well. Wasting no time, she proceeded to sue the plastic surgeon for a breach of contract; he had told her that he would perform the operation himself. Indeed, her only reason for consulting this particular surgeon was because of his excellent reputation for performing this very operation. She won her case and was awarded damages.

In the form which is recommended, the patient gives consent for further or alternative operative measures as may be found necessary. An example of this could be a patient admitted with severe abdominal pain who is taken to theatre for laparotomy. Any one of a number of procedures may become necessary, based on the findings at laparatomy, e.g. bowel resection or appendicectomy. It is most unlikely that any surgeon would take this statement to indicate that he is given *carte blanche*: This is particularly true regarding mutilating operations (e.g. amputation, mastectomy); it is equally true of operations such as colostomy or ileostomy. Except in an emergency, the procedure will be explained to the patient, allowing him time to come to terms with the situation. Some hospitals employ stoma therapists and counsellors who visit the patient pre-operatively to give practical and psychological support and advice.

When informed consent has been given it will apply only to an operation on a particular date; it does not automatically constitute consent to further operations. A patient admitted for dilatation and curretage may, as the result of the findings, require hysterectomy. In this case, the operation will be explained to her by the surgeon and a further consent requested.

**Consent in Emergency Situations**

There is no black and white ruling regarding consent for emergency surgery, certainly not in the case of a rational,

conscious patient of full age. While the surgeon has a professional duty to do all that is reasonably possible to preserve life,
the patient has got every right to refuse treatment if he so wishes.
It is uncommon, however, for this situation to arise.

## Summary

The issue of consent is assuming increasing importance in Britain.
Time was when the doctor did whatever he thought best for the
patient – who was eternally grateful, whatever the outcome. As a
student nurse, many years ago, I have presented many surgical
patients with the traditional piece of paper and asked them to
sign. I cannot ever remember asking them to read it first; it was
no more than a formality: But times have changed; patients are
now more informed of their rights and we, as nurses, must be one
step ahead, with up-to-date knowledge of what we can and
cannot do.

No consent can ever be totally informed; if it were, it would be
necessary to explain every conceivable detail of the proposed
procedure together with even unlikely side-effects, previous
results and possible prognosis to the patient. If this were done,
then it is unlikely that many people would submit to surgery;
there has got to be an element of trust.

Decision-making with regard to treatment is the surgeon's
province; the nurse simply carries it out. However, if she is to be
considered as a professional she must recognise that the giving of
any treatment without the patient's consent can constitute assault
and battery, both civil wrongs and criminal offences.

## References

1. Joe Jacob, *Speller's Law Relating to Hospitals and Kindred Institutions*, 6th ed. H.K. Lewis & Co, 1978. Ch. 13, Consent to treatment
   and kindred matters, pp. 182-6; Appendix E: Operations and other
   procedures, Forms of consent.
2. D.J. Gee, *Lecture Notes on Forensic Medicine*, Blackwell Scientific
   Publications, 3rd ed., 1979, Ch. 5.
3. Family Law Reform Act 1969.
4. Taylor J. Leahy (ed.), *Medical Malpractice*, Wright, 1980, p. 171.

# 4 OBJECTIONS TO SURGERY

Why should any patient object, if it is advised by the surgeon that an operation is the best course of treatment to relieve a particular conditon? Surely the surgeon, as a professional, must know best? Many nurses become extremely annoyed when patients decide, for one reason or another, not to have an operation. They argue that hospitalisation costs time and money and nowhere is this more apparent than in the theatre. Instruments are sterilised and prepared, the nurse is 'scrubbed', the list is organised, and then there is a message that the patient has changed his mind.

Some patients are ill-informed about the proposed operation on admission, and it may be that in talking with nursing staff and other patients that they actually learn exactly the implications of their particular operation. Other patients lack courage to argue or disagree with the doctor and it is only when the actual time to go to theatre arrives that they decide to voice their objection. The problem of patients who speak little or no English is always with us, and at times, insufficient attention is paid to this. Britain is now a cosmopolitan country and, whatever the difficulty, it is essential that an interpreter is found to explain the proposed operation to many of our patients.

## Who Can Object to Surgery?

Any conscious adult patient of sound mind, in any circumstance.

## Who Cannot Object to Surgery?

An unconscious patient or one who is so affected by his physical condition as to be in no state of mind either to consent or object.[1]

Democracy is characterised by the maintenance of fundamental freedoms for the ordinary individual and this freedom is embodied in the Common Law and is assured by Magna Carta.[2]

Any invasion of this freedom would destroy the very foundation of liberty which protects each person from injury by another, subject only to constitutionally made laws. Democracy is a way of life in the Western world, and it therefore follows that in Britain individual freedom of choice is a right and only in exceptional circumstances can it be taken away.

Patients requiring elective surgery are neither morally nor legally bound to submit to it; they have a choice. The surgeon's duty is to explain the proposed treatment, which, in his opinion, is most likely to improve the patient's condition. If the patient decides against the treatment the surgeon has a further duty to explain the possible consequences of this refusal, but the patient must not be pressurised or persuaded to submit to treatment against his will. This would be an infringement of his rights.

We encounter one of the many complexities of the Law when discussing a patient's objection to surgery. While on the one hand it is acknowledged that a patient has, of right, a choice, on the other hand, the surgeon has a professional duty to do all he can to preserve life. It may even be that if he is seen to fail in this duty by allowing a patient to die, from choice, a charge of manslaughter could be made.

The word 'law' implies the idea of order, involving a set of rules prescribed by Parliament, and as such is often called the rule of law. But this law cannot exist in the abstract; it is influenced by the general state of culture of the people and to a great extent is determined by existing standards. These standards may be determined by moral law, which is concerned with conduct, natural law, knowing right from wrong, and divine and ethical law, which for the believer are interrelated. Ethics, too, may be a material basis for positive law.

**Religious Objections**

For a number of patients, their objection to surgery, in any circumstance, will be based on a strongly-held religious belief. In the busy life of a hospital it is extremely difficult for doctor or nurse to be aware of the religion of every patient and of any doctrines held by that religion which may affect treatment. The most common problem for patients is the depersonalisation process to which they are subjected, and this is particularly true for the surgical patient. While every effort is made to respect his dignity, the efficiency of the service usually comes first. Undoubtedly, the practice of the Nursing Process will solve many of these problems, when the visiting theatre nurse and the ward staff will have allowed time to sit and talk with each patient, discovering not only information about their illness but also details of cultural and religious beliefs.

The nurse must be constantly aware of the temptation to form judgements of her patients, basing these on her own cultural or religious beliefs. All patients must be treated with the same respect and there will be times when this can be extremely difficult, as with a patient who refuses blood transfusion, knowing that this action will hasten their death.

Compulsory reading for all nurses is *Second Life* by Stephani Cook.[3] It is a brilliant autobiography of a young woman who was subjected to some, hopefully, rare indignities during an unnecessarily long stay in hospital and it highlights just how easy it can be to become insensitive to a patient's very basic needs.

Christianity is the dominant religion in Britain, but respect for the particular religious beliefs of all patients should be seen in the context as no more than a continuation of care. The particular beliefs of a variety of religions are given here, together with attitudes to medical or surgical treatment.

### Jehovah's Witnesses

Much has been written about the objection of particular religious groups — notably Jehovah's Witnesses — to surgery. This is in fact a misconception; they do not object to surgery, elective or emergency, but to transfusion of human blood. They accept modern medical treatment and many of them are doctors. They view blood as sacred and base their refusal on the following scripture:

> Every moving thing that liveth shall be meat for you: even as the green herb have I given you all things. But the flesh with the life thereof, which is the blood thereof, ye shall not eat. (Genesis 9:34)

> For it (the blood) is the life of all flesh; the blood of it is for the life thereof: therefore I say unto the children of Israel, Ye shall eat the blood of no manner of flesh: for the life of all

flesh is the blood thereof: whosoever eateth it shall be cut off. (Leviticus 17: 14)

For it seemed to the Holy Ghost and to us, to lay upon you no greater burden than these necessary things; that ye abstain from meats offered to idols, and from blood, and from things strangled and from fornication; from which if ye keep yourselves ye shall do well. (Acts 15:19,20)

Simply be firmly resolved not to eat blood, because the blood is the soul and you must not eat the soul with the flesh. You must not eat it. You should pour it out upon the ground as water. (Deuteronomy 12:23,24)

Witnesses also maintain that refusing blood and requesting alternative therapies may have medical advantages and they believe that many new procedures and trends in 'bloodless' surgery have only come about because of doctors looking for better ways to operate on Jehovah's Witnesses.

## Christian Scientists

The doctrine of this church is that healing of physical diseases must be brought about only by spiritual means. Sickness and sin are seen as errors of the human mind and can be eliminated by altering thoughts, not by drugs or medicines. Hypnotism or any form of psychotherapy are not allowed and alcohol, coffee and tobacco are seen as drugs and must not be used. The church operates several nursing homes which rely solely on spiritual healing. Blood transfusion or drugs are not accepted, physical examination or biopsies are not allowed and vaccines are accepted only when required by law. There are no Last Rites and autopsy is allowed only in cases of sudden death.

Christian Scientists may be admitted to National Health hospitals for:

(1) Childbirth: A doctor or qualified midwife must be in attendance by law.
(2) Fractures: A surgeon may set bones.
(3) Infectious diseases: Such diseases are reported to the proper authorities and patients are willing to be isolated, if necessary.

## Objections to Surgery

(4) Lack of finance: Christian Scientists who can no longer afford treatment in their own nursing homes, despite financial help, may decide to use NHS facilities.

(5) Lack of faith: Those whose faith is not strong enough to believe that a cure can be effected by spiritual means may seek alternative treatment. This particular faith is based on Genesis 1:26:6 'And God said, "Let us make man, wearing our own image and likeness" '; and Paul in Ephesians 4 where he states the need to put off the old man of imperfect material and put on the new man, which is after God.

### Adventists

No stated objection to surgery but stimulants, narcotics and hypnosis are forbidden.

### American Indians

All have religious magic, folklore and herbal disease treatment. Medicine men and conjurers in various tribes perform by use of many different symbolic actions against illnesses, social taboos, powers of nature and enemy-oriented disease. Today, many Indians follow modern Christian religions while some continue with their Indian beliefs.

### Armenians

No conflict between modern medicine and religion.

### Baha'i

No conflict between modern medicine and religion. The sick are specifically instructed in Baha'i scripture to seek the advice of competent doctors. Spiritual health is felt to be conducive to physical health.

### Baptists

Most Baptists believe that God works through the doctor but some may be resistant to medical treatment. Some who believe in predestination respond passively to care.

### Buddhists

Buddists are in harmony with modern science. They believe that illness is a trial to develop the soul but have no conflict with modern medicine. Some Buddhists may be distressed by the use of drugs which reduce consciousness, since importance is often placed upon the conscious state of mind at death. They have a number of special holy days during the year and, if possible, patients should be questioned as to their feelings about having medical or surgical treatment on those days.

## Hindus

It is extremely important to the Hindu patient that he is allowed to practise his religion in hospital. Hindus believe in the transmigration of the soul, one's next life being dependent on behaviour in this life. Although they do not object to necessary treatment, some conditions, such as loss of a limb, represent sins committed in a previous life. Cleanliness is very important to Hindus, and they have particular washing rituals. Dietary rules forbid the eating of beef, and pork is not usually acceptable. Certain prescribed rites are carried out by the Hindu priest after death. Hindus are particular about who touches the body, which is normally washed by the family. Married women and children may wear red markings on the forehead. Married women may also wear a 'nuptial' thread/necklace, and male adults a 'sacred thread' on the arm or body. These should be worn continually, and should remain on the body at death. Hindus find autopsy abhorrent and cremation is the normal mode of disposal.

## Muslims

Followers of Islam often have a fatalistic view that can militate against ready compliance with therapy but there is no stated objection to surgery. According to Islamic practice, circumcision is compulsory for hygienic purposes and is usually performed on boys between the ages of 10-12. A strict segregation of the sexes is observed so that many Asian women may be found resistant to uncovering the body or to physical contact and they may react adversely to examination by a male doctor. Asian dress has a religious significance; it is meant to cover all of the body including the legs so some women may be reluctant to wear Western-style nightdresses or pyjamas.

If abortion occurs before 130 days the foetus is treated as any other discarded tissue but after 130 days an aborted foetus must be treated as a fully developed human being and, unlike under

British custom, it is expected that there will be a funeral ceremony. At the moment a child is born it is the custom to make the *Athan*, a call to prayer, so that these are the first words the child will hear. The *Athan* can be made by the father and it is most important that staff accede to this request, if possible.

Dietary rules forbid the eating of pork, bacon or ham of any description, and any food cooked in or containing lard. Alcohol is allowed only as a constituent of medication.

Fasting is an obligatory religious act and Muslims must fast during all the hours of daylight during the month of Ramadan. This is the ninth month of the Islamic year and usually corresponds to August/September. Patients in hospital can be exempt from this fasting but some Muslims may still wish to observe the ritual. At death, the family wash and prepare the body; a woman's body should be washed by a Muslim woman and a man's body by a Muslim man. The corpse must face Mecca (i.e. south-east). Once the body has been washed and prepared it must remain untouched. Post-mortem is allowed only if required by law and no body parts should be removed.

## Sikhs

No stated objection to surgery. For male patients, hair and beard should remain uncut. If hair is shaved for surgical purposes, a Sikh will need to be readmitted to his religion. The turban has a religious significance but many Sikhs in Britain have abandoned wearing it. Male religious Sikhs wear shorts, steel bracelet, steel dagger and a steel comb and these should remain on the body after death.

Strict Sikhs are prohibited from eating beef in any form and some are total vegetarians. Autopsy is abhorrent to Sikhs and cremation rather than burial is the norm.

## Greek Orthodox

No stated objection to surgery. Religious dietary rules prescribe a fast period which means avoidance of meat and dairy products. These rules need not be enforced in cases of illness but some patients may insist on fasting. If this would adversely affect treatment a priest should be called to convince the patient to forgo fasting.

It is the belief of the Greek Orthodox Church that every reasonable effort should be made to preserve life until it is terminated by God and euthanasia and termination of pregnancy are opposed. Autopsies are discouraged and burial is preferred to cremation.

## Mormons (Church of Jesus Christ of Latter-day Saints)

Devout adherents believe in divine healing through the 'laying on of hands', but many do not prohibit medical therapy. In the USA, the Church maintains an extensive and well-funded welfare system, including financial support for the sick. Alcoholic drinks, tobacco, hot drinks (tea, coffee) or any other substance which may be injurious to the body are prohibited. Cremation is discouraged and baptism of the dead is essential.

## Quakers (Friends)

No restrictions on medical treatment and individual members are allowed to make their own decisions. Most practise moderation in diet, avoiding drugs and alcohol. They are pacifists and conscientious objectors and do not believe in life after death.

## Pentecostals (Assembly of God Foursquare Church)

No objection to blood transfusion or medical care. Believe in the possibility of divine healing through prayer. Abstain from alcohol, tobacco and eating strangled animals or any food to which blood has been added. Individuals may refuse pork.

## Roman Catholics

No objection to surgery or blood transfusion. Church doctrine forbids termination of pregnancy. Infant baptism is mandatory and is especially urgent if prognosis is poor. If amputation of a limb is performed, the patient or a relative may request that it be buried in consecrated ground. The Sacrament of the Sick was formerly referred to as the 'Last Rites' or Last Sacrament, and this led people to believe that it was the final act of faith in life. In fact it is intended for recovery of health or for grace to suffer and the doctrine for this sacrament is taken from James 5:14-15: 'Is any sick among you? Let him call for the elders of the Church and let them pray for him, anointing him with oil in the name of the Lord. And the prayer of faith shall save the sick, and the Lord shall raise him up; And if he hath committed sins, they shall be forgiven him.' The patient or relatives may request the priest to administer the Sacrament of the Sick.

## Objections to Surgery

### Russian Orthodox

No objection to surgery. It is important that male patients are not shaved, the only exception being for surgery. Members wear a cross necklace and it should be replaced immediately after surgery. At death, the arms should be crossed and fingers set in a cross. Clothing at death must be of natural fibre so that the body will change to dust sooner. The Church does not believe in autopsies, embalming or cremation.

### Jews

Members of this faith constitute slightly under 1% of the total population of Britain. In belief and practice they vary between Orthodox and Liberal (or Reform). There is no stated objection to surgery, but some Jews may refuse surgery during Shabbat (the sabbath), unless assured by a rabbi that this treatment is medically necessary at this time. Strict kosher dietary laws are adhered to by observant Jews and nursing staff should be aware of the importance of this to the patient. It may be impossible for a general hospital to supply this food and many Jewish patients rely on food being brought in by friends or relatives. When a patient dies, many Jews prefer to wash and prepare the body themselves. If a Jew dies on the sabbath the body is left until the Sabbath is ended and it is usual for a relative to sit and mourn over the body until the time for burial, which is usually 24 hours after death.

Many Jews adhere strictly to the rules of the sabbath which state that no work of any kind is to be carried out on that day: 'Six days shalt thou labour, and do all thy work. But the seventh day is the sabbath of the Lord thy God; in it thou shalt not do any work . . .' (Exodus 20:9-10). The sabbath runs from sundown on Friday to sundown on Saturday and a Jewish patient who is due for discharge during this time may request discharge either before Friday evening or on Sunday. Organs or other body tissue may be requested by the family for burial and donation or transplantation of organs requires permission of a rabbi.

Within each religion there will be individuals and sects whose beliefs and teachings are different from those described above. Whether a patient be atheist, agnostic of a particular religious affiliation or none at all, this information should be available to all staff caring for him; it can affect his attitude towards treatment and his recovery rate. In many cases this information will be of value to mortuary technicians. Included in the ICN Code for Nurses is the statement 'The nurse, in providing care, promotes an environment in which the values, customs and spiritual beliefs of the individual are respected'.

### Jehovah's Witness refused blood

A Jehovah's Witness died four months after he refused a blood transfusion, an inquest heard. Roy Bell told the Southwark Coroner that his father . . . had been admitted to Lewisham Hospital in May for a drink problem . . . 'Doctors at the hospital wanted to perform a blood transfusion but our religion does not allow this so my father refused the operation,' he said . . . Summing up, Sir Montague Levine said, 'This man suffered a major haemorrhage due to sclerosis of the liver and I don't think his refusing the operation had a direct bearing on his death'.[4]

A Jehovah's Witness couple in Sicily whose child died after they refused to allow blood transfusions have been charged with manslaughter.[5]

This case in Sicily is an interesting one. The parents were arrested on 5 July 1980 and charged with voluntary homicide and imprisoned for 20 months to await trial. On 10 March 1982 they were tried and found guilty. A sentence of 14 years in prison, followed by three years' probation, was imposed. I have been informed by the Watch Tower Bible and Tract Society, London, that the sentence was reduced at a subsequent appeal but a further appeal is being prepared to be presented to a higher court in Rome.[6]

### Objection to Surgery by a Spouse

Emmeline Pankhurst and her husband, a barrister, drafted the Married Women's Property Act of 1882 and they founded the Women's Franchise League in 1889. Mrs Pankhurst was the leader of the militant 'suffragettes' and was imprisoned eight times for her sensational activities on behalf of the rights of women, an interest which consumed her until the time of her death in 1928. The fight was continued by her daughter, Christabel, and their efforts contributed in no small way to the granting of the vote to women in 1918.

The Married Women's Property Act was enacted for the protection of women; before this Act, by common law, a husband, on marriage, became entitled to all the personal property which his wife had, or later acquired, and his rights even extended to her earnings. This Act allowed a married woman to hold separate property and to enter into contracts. The Act also made a husband responsible for his wife's pre-marriage debts and any tort committed by her (this last section of the Act was removed in 1935).

The struggle for the emancipation of women has continued to this day and the Equal Pay Act 1970 and the Sex Discrimination Act 1975 are but two pieces of legislation resultant from this struggle. In the church marriage service, the word 'obey' has now dissapeared – yet further theoretical evidence of the equality of the sexes.

Yet another complexity of the Law is encountered when a married woman requires or requests surgery which will affect her reproductive capacity, but her legal/common law husband objects. What rights, if any, has the husband got in this matter? There are two answers to this question; firstly, if the operation is medically necessary, only the consent of the patient is required. As in all other cases, the surgeon will explain the proposed operation to the patient, outlining the expected result, e.g. hysterectomy, the inability to have children. In ordinary circumstances, when the patient is living with her husband the surgeon will, if requested, also explain the result of the procedure to the husband; but this will be a matter of politeness and not a legal requirement.[7]

Secondly, if a married woman requests the operation on social grounds (and this also applies in the case of the husband), consent of the partner is necessary, if the operation 'permanently or possibly permanently takes away the capacity for childbearing or procreation'.[8] 'Any operation done without medical need, which necessarily resulted in serious injury to the person on whom it was performed, or had more than a minimal probability of doing so, could lay the person who performed it open to the risk of prosecution, the consent of the person injured being no defence in such circumstances'; and 'the only procedures likely to be carried out by a registered medical practitioner, is sterilisation of a patient of either sex otherwise than on medical grounds, the sterilisation being undertaken at the request of the person sterilised, and cosmetic surgery'.[9]

## Objection to Surgery by Parent/Guardian

It is normal practice to obtain permission from a parent before operating on a child and in the majority of cases, elective or emergency, this does not pose any problem. If the parent brings the child to hospital for treatment – surgical or medical – then there is normally no reason why the treatment should not be accepted. Whenever I ask nurses what procedure the doctor should follow if parents object to surgery on their child in an emergency situation, they inevitably answer 'get a Court order to overrule the objection'. While it is true that in certain circumstances a doctor has the legal right to do this, in practice it is rarely necessary. The picture of the doctor as an ogre or dictator is not one which will endear him to any patient and the few occasions on which is it necessary for him to obtain a Court order are instanced by the fact that they are well publicised by the press.

Take the case of parents in their 40s; they have one child that they waited for in their 20-year marriage and this 'wonder' baby was born when the mother was 40. The baby has been 'sickly' since birth but he has become the centre of his parents' life, their reason for living. At the age of two years he requires major surgery, for which, as in all cases, the surgeon cannot give any guarantee that the child will recover from the anaesthetic, let alone the operation. Is it not understandable that the parents are reluctant to give their consent for surgery? Another instance might be where a child has had repeated surgery since birth for a congenital abnormality. Caring for him has become a burden for the parents; their marriage is in difficulty; the other children in the family are neglected and have become resentful and the whole structure of the family has been damaged. Will getting a Court order in this situation really solve any problem? Medical decisions are rarely based solely on legal considerations; moral and ethical values together with what is best for the individual patient will influence most decisions made by doctors. This of course is not to say that they can practise outside the Law, but as professionals they cannot apply rules rigidly when each case obviously has its unique aspects.

If a child is admitted, unconscious, to hospital and he requires immediate surgery, no doctor would be considered irresponsible if he gives whatever treatment is necessary, irrespective of whether consent has been sought/given or refused.

When parents offer an objection to surgery on their child it is the duty of the doctor to explain carefully the possible consequences of this action. If it is possible to defer the operation, it should not be performed against the wishes of the parents. In the last analysis, the decision rests with the doctor, and if time allows, he will consult with a senior colleague before making his decision.

It is appropriate that her name was Claire Light. Her name shone as a brilliant beacon through a week of grown-up petulance and tantrums. Tragically, her life was short. Worse, for all her 13 valiant years she fought against cancer. Shortly before Easter she decided against any further medical treatment. The poor kid had had enough. 'It is my body' she told her mother at their Cardiff home. 'I shall do it my way'. Claire drew out her savings and bought mother a silver tray. Then she sent this notice to the local newspaper: I would like to thank all the doctors and nurses at the Heath and Llandough Hospitals for taking care of me when I was ill. And many thanks to those special friends and relatives who have been so kind. Also the Heath Hospital Lourdes Group who took me to Lourdes. Also my Mam and Dad, sister Shirl and brother Andy. Love Claire.[10]

Reporting this, Philip Wrack wrote:

Professor Peter Grey did his talented, loving best to save young Claire. Alas it was not to be. The Professor said 'she was very young to take the decision to refuse more operations and treatment but that was the sort of girl she was — courageous and brave. Claire left the world a better place than she had found it'.

## Parent's Objection to Termination of Pregnancy on a Child

The Abortion Act 1967 allows for the lawful termination of a pregnancy, up to 28 weeks, subject to the conditions of the Act. The 28-week limit is protected by the Infant Life (Preservation) Act 1929. This Act states that it is an offence to destroy the life of a child capable of being born alive and that after the 28th week of the pregnancy it shall *prima facie* be presumed that the child was capable of being born. The provisions of this Act do not apply if the foetus was destroyed in good faith for the purpose of preserving the life of the mother. The Medical Defence Union advise 'that in the case of a girl under 16 years requiring termination of pregnancy, her parents should always be consulted, but that their refusal of consent should not prevent clinically necessary termination of pregnancy to which the patient herself has consented' and 'conversely, a termination should never be carried out in opposition to the girl's wishes even if the parents demand it'.[11]

## Objection by Wife to Removal of Husband's Male Organs and Fashioning of Artificial Vagina

The view is expressed in *Law Relating to Hospitals* (Forms of consent) that it is questionable whether the operation should be performed without the consent of the wife. It is reported that 'many trans-sexuals have attempted to live as their congenital sex, marrying and having children' but 'one of the criteria to be met before being referred to a surgeon is that the trans-sexual must be single or divorced'.[12]

## Objection by Mentally Ill or Mentally Handicapped Patients to Treatment

The Mental Health (Amendment) Act 1982 came into effect on 1st September 1983 and it replaces the Mental Health Act (1959) and the Mental Health (Scotland) Act 1960. Section 44 (3) states:

subject to section 48, a patient shall not be given any form of treatment to which this section applies unless – (a) he has consented to that treatment and either the responsible medical officer or a medical practitioner appointed for the purposes of this part of this Act by the Secretary of State has certified in writing that the patient is capable of understanding its nature, purpose and likely effects and has consented to it; or (b) a medical practitioner . . . has certified in writing that the patient is not capable of understanding the nature, purpose and likely effects of that treatment or has not consented to it but that, having regard to the likelihood of its alleviating or preventing a deterioration of his condition, the treatment should be given.

### Objection by Patients to be Used for Teaching or Research

It is reasonable for patients to understand that during the course of necessary treatment, they may serve as teaching material for students — medical or nursing — in hospital. Certainly from the nursing viewpoint, most nursing treatment in hospital is given by students — basic or post-basic — and it is only by 'using' the patient as a model that nursing skills are perfected. It is the responsibility of the sister to ensure that the student is instructed and supervised but it is the student who has to carry out the particular task, time and time again, in order to master the skill, e.g. giving an intramuscular injection. An orange may serve as a model in the classroom but sooner or later she will have to start with 'the real thing': a living patient who reacts to pain or discomfort.

There are many patients who believe that they cannot refuse any treatment in hospital and some are just too frightened to voice an objection; however, the majority co-operate in treatment and are tolerant and even encouraging to the student. It is common courtesy and also good nursing practice to explain any treatment to the patient and then invite his co-operation, e.g. giving an intravenous injection in the anaesthetic room. Of course it will be the anaesthetist who will be giving this injection but either he or the anaesthetic nurse will briefly explain what is happening to the patient and then ask him to extend his arm. By virtue of doing this, the patient gives consent to treatment. The students who are present are therefore learning by observation. The DHSS circular *Teaching on Patients* (HMSO (73) 8,) explains that all patients should be told that they may refuse to be used for teaching but that their refusal will in no way prejudice their treatment.

## Research

It could be said that all patient treatment is experimental; no two patients necessarily react to a particular treatment in the same way, however well-established the treatment might be. In the context in which the word research is used here, it refers to a procedure designed for gaining information and does not refer to any treatment which is primarily designed to treat a condition, but which, incidentally, produces new information which might be of value in developing or perfecting an existing treatment or procedure.

The position on consent varies according to whether the research is expected to be of benefit to the patient or not.

Where no benefit to the individual patient is expected a full explanation of the proposed procedure should be given and the patient must feel completely free to decline to participate or to withdraw at any stage. This should usually be in the presence of a witness. Where research is intended to benefit the patient, although consent should ordinarily be sought, there are sometimes circumstances in which it is inappropriate or even inhumane to explain the details and seek consent. Ethical committees should examine such cases with particular care.[13]

Do you, the reader, know if there is an Ethical Committee in your hospital? It could be a very useful source of information.

*The Practitioner* reviews a case where the patient was a participant in a randomised controlled trial. At the inquest it was revealed not only that there had been an apparent failure to follow laid down procedure, but also that throughout the United Kingdom patients had unknowingly been selected for participation in potentially dangerous drug trials without consent of, or consultation with, themselves or their families. In this particular trial the decision not to ask for consent had been passed by ethical committees in 11 different areas . . .[14]

### Objection to Female Circumcision

I deal here, not with patient's objections, but with the objection of nurses to being involved in this practice. Female circumcision is a ritual, carried out mainly in certain African countries, and is performed there, without anaesthetic, on females from babyhood to middle age. As yet, there is no legislation in the UK which forbids the performance of this operation, except on medical grounds, but a Bill proposed by Lord Kennet to ban this operation in Britain received total support and has now begun its parliamentary passage through the Lords. The proposed Bill has the backing of the Royal College of Nursing. I can only say at this stage, that any nurse who is asked to be a party to this procedure, which many people consider a barbaric and inhumane practice, should think well before becoming involved, take advice from her senior manager and professional organisation, and for her own protection, ascertain her legal position. If the proposed legislation is not accepted it may be that nurses will be given the choice of 'opting out' of the procedure.

### Summary

The traditional view in Western society is that illness is an unacceptable intrusion on our lives and it must be treated or cured as soon as possible. It therefore follows that we, as nurses, can become conditioned to seeing our role as 'curers' rather than 'carers' and the patient as no more than an accepting automaton. In our busy working life, we may find that the patient who either questions or objects to treatment can easily become labelled as a trouble-maker. While we cannot hope to take the words of Florence Nightingale too literally when she said 'all patients should be treated as honoured guests', we must avoid placing limitations on their freedom to act and think independently.

It would be neither possible nor practical to talk about the Law for doctors and nurses separately in relation to patients' objections to surgery. As professionals, we must ensure that we are sufficiently knowledgeable about the infinite variety of factors which influence individual beliefs and decisions and it is only in doing this that we can hope to care for the patient as a 'whole' person.

The Law is not a tyrant but we must not be carried away in the belief that it is automatically on our side because we have the power to impose ourselves on hospital patients. Sensitivity to their needs and the effort to understand their views, however unreasonable they may seem, will foster a mutual respect and this in turn should help to avoid situations where the patient's rights are ignored.

## References

1. Joe Jacob, *Speller's Law Relating to Hospitals and Kindred Institutions*, 6th ed. H.K. Lewis & Co, 1978. Ch. 13, Consent to treatment and kindred matters, p. 190 (d).
2. Magna Carta 1215, reissue 1225.
3. Stephani Cook, *Second Life*, Michael Joseph, 1982.
4. 'Jehovah's Witness refused blood', *South London Press*, 14 October 1980.
5. *Daily Express*, 2 March 1982.
6. 'A shocking injustice', *Awake!*, Watch Tower Bible and Tract Society, London, 22 October 1982.
7. Joe Jacob, *Speller's Law*, Ch. 13, Married persons (a), pp. 202-4.
8. Ibid., Ch. 13, Married persons (b), pp. 203-4.
9. Ibid., Ch. 13, Illegal operations (b), p. 209.
10. Philip Wrack, Sunday Punchline, *News of the World*, 19 June 1983.
11. Joe Jacob, *Speller's Law*, Appendix E: Operations and other procedures, Forms of consent, Girls under 16.
12. Kate Campbell, 'A woman in the making', *Nursing Mirror*, 18 August 1983.
13. *Patients' Rights*, National Consumer Council, London 1982. (HSC(1S) 153 DHHS 1975. Supervision of the ethics of clinical research investigation and fetal research, para. 3; quoting from a 1973 report of the Royal College of Physicians on supervision of ethics of clinical research investigations in institutions.)
14. *Nursing Times*, 15 December 1982, Research digest, p. 2122. (From D. Brahams in *The Practitioner*, 1982, 226: pp. 1829-30.)

Much useful information on religious objections to surgery has been obtained from the following publications:

J.M.F. Clarke, 'Surgery in Jehovah's Witnesses', *British Journal of Hospital Medicine*, May 1982, pp. 497-500.

Alix Henley and Jim Clayton, 'Religion of the Muslims', *Health and Social Services Journal*, 29 July 1982, pp. 918-19.

Edward Martin, Guy's Hospital Chaplaincy, *Notes on Religious Needs of Patients* (unpublished notes for use of Guy's Hospital).

'Beliefs that can affect therapy', *Pediatric Nusing*, May-June 1979, pp.

40-3 (from *Nursing Update*, July 1975).

Rev. John B. Pumphrey (prepared in consultation with), 'Reorganising your patient's spiritual needs', *Nursing* (US), December 1977, pp. 64-9.

Rev. Dennis Saylor, 'The spiritual self', *Journal of Practical Nursing*, August 1977, pp. 16-17, 30.

Caroline Walker, 'Attitudes to death and bereavement among cultural minority groups', *Nursing Times*, 15 December 1982, pp. 2106-9.

# 5  LACK OF COMMUNICATION

I know you think you understand what you think I said, but I
am not sure you realise that what you heard is what I meant.

Anonymous

'Sir, I am glad to say that my husband, reported missing, is
now dead.'
'Please find out if my husband is dead, as the man I am now
living with won't eat or do anything until he is sure.'
'My doctor has had me in bed for a week now, but it doesn't
seem to be doing me any good.'
'Unless I get my Husband's money, I shall be forced to lead an
immortal life.'

The above extracts from letters sent to the Pension Office are
certainly crude, but it is not too difficult to work out what the
writers really meant.

Nurses working in the wards have the advantage of being able
to move freely among the patients, chatting as they make their
beds or feed them. They wear a distinctive uniform, do not
normally wear masks and generally have a distinct advantage
over the theatre nurse. There are many barriers to communication in the operating theatre, not least the very fact that it is a
unit in isolation and the obvious need to control the number of
people entering the department.

The employing authority is responsible for ensuring that the
staff it employs meet established criteria – character, health,
qualifications and proficiency in written and spoken English. The
theatre manager is responsible for selecting trained staff and the
Education Division is responsible for selecting students at basic
and post-basic level. Therefore it seems reasonable to start with
the premise that all the nursing staff will understand each other.
But is this indeed reasonable?

The EEC nursing directives became operative on 29 June
1979, allowing registered nurses freedom of movement to work in
one or other of the member states. The General Nursing Council
is responsible for operating the EEC nursing directives in

England and Wales and for dealing with applications for documentation from nurses trained in the UK who intend seeking recognition in other EEC countries. Nurses from other EEC countries who wish to work in the UK must satisfy the prospective employing authority about their competence in English.

Student nurses are expected to have an 'O' level GCE in English before being accepted for training and during the following three years their educational programme will gradually introduce them to the language and nomenclature of medicine and nursing. Bearing this in mind, it is inevitable that there will be communication problems for the overseas nurse working in the operating theatre.

Heidi Weinrich, a German working as a staff nurse at St George's Hospital, Tooting, said:

> When I came to London, I discovered that my basic knowledge of English was not sufficient to understand nursing and medical terms. It took me a good two weeks to more or less follow the ward report. The hospital seemed a labyrinth where I had to find my way through. The totally different nursing system and its organisation were difficult to understand. The many different levels in the hierarchy and the 'Who's Who' were unknown to me. I was not used to the very official behaviour between everybody.[1]

Theatre nursing relies heavily on communication – verbal and non-verbal – and being able to read and write a language does not automatically guarantee that one can speak it. Apart from the language of medicine and nursing, often spiced with highly technical terms, there are local accents, regional dialects and the colloquial form of language. How would you deal with the Cockney patient who arrives in theatre complaining that because he couldn't find his 'Cape of Good Hope' (soap) he couldn't have a 'dig in the grave' (shave)?

A most dangerous practice, which unfortunately seems to be routine in many theatres, is the use of abbreviations. The Joint Memoranda of the Medical Defence Union and the Royal College of Nursing, 'Safeguards against wrong operations', states 'the operation list should be typed and photocopied and should show the *nature* [my italics] of the operation and the patient's full name and hospital number', and 'all reference to the operation type or site should be written in full'. Here is a sample operation list:

D&C   Ts&As   ERPC   TAH   BSO   EUA   DPNS   CABG
THR   TUR[2]

Is it likely that all staff involved in the care of the surgical patient will understand this or will this blatant disregard of the recommendations lead to confusion, a lack of communication and possible accidents to patients? It is sad that professionals deliberately misuse language and demean it with total disregard for patient safety.

Effective communication really is vital in theatre and is improved or hindered by the amount of attention paid to everything we do.

At 49, Mr Patrick McCann was a healthy man when he went into hospital, the Walsgrove, Coventry. He left there in a box after an operation for cancer; but he did not have the disease. There was a mix-up in tests taken from another patient. At the inquest, a consultant pathologist stated that an independent inquiry had established there could not possibly be any improvement on the 'excellent' safety measures at the hospital.

Reporting this case in the *News of the World*, John Field commented: 'That to my mind is a load of codswallop'.[3]

How easy it is to get specimens mixed up – a busy list of dilatation and curretages with perhaps specimens from every patient. We cannot possibly rely on memory to identify individual specimens when confronted with a row of identical specimen jars. Each specimen must be labelled as soon as it is collected; a patient's life may depend on it.

Quite rightly, great emphasis is placed on establishing a foolproof method of identifying patients in theatre and in ensuring that the correct operation is performed. The Joint Memoranda 'Safeguards against wrong operations' states: 'mistakes may occur when changes are made in the theatre lists after the start of the operating session, particularly if such changes have not been notified to all concerned immediately they have been made. Operation lists should be altered as little as possible and never by telephone.'

HOSPITAL GETS WRONG OP RAP

Hospital staff have been rapped for carrying out a stomach operation on a boy who was admitted for minor ear surgery. The blunder was only spotted when seven-year-old John Burley was recovering afterwards at Bromsgrove General Hospital, Worcs. But an inquiry set up by the area health authority says a senior sister, junior nurse, anaesthetist and surgeon all failed to realise the operation was being carried out on the wrong boy. They confused him with another boy, also called John, who DID need stomach surgery. The report blames the mix-up on lack of communication between staff, and the pressures of working in an old and overcrowded hospital.

In a bid to prevent future blunders, it urges a new system of putting name labels on patients. It also says the area of an operation should be marked on a patient's body before going for surgery. The report says the boy did not suffer any harm from the operation for umbilical hernia.[4]

Given similar circumstances this mistake might have happened in any theatre.

An enquiry has begun at a hospital in Vienna into how a man, suffering from a broken leg, was mistakenly given a heart pacemaker.[5]

Nurses caring for surgical patients endeavour to give devoted, conscientious and effective service, but they too are human and the criticism to which they are sometimes subjected often seems to be uninformed and savours of ingratitude. The nurse's contact with the patient is more continuous than the doctor's and treating the patient as a living being – not just a case – is one of the most powerful aids to communication. We must learn to *listen*, not just to patients but to each other. It is so easy to believe that 'the work' is all-important, applying intense concentration on the physical tasks in hand but giving scant attention to the actual patient. By doing this we are, in fact, communicating either that we are disinterested or we just haven't got time. We should reflect on this daily.

Non-verbal communication comes into its own in theatre: the scrub team, covered in sterilised gowns, screaming silently, 'don't touch!' As in every other similar situation the message will not get through to many staff until there is an induction programme for all new staff. Many mistakes could be avoided if even the basic 'do's and don'ts' of theatre were taught to every new member of staff of all grades.

Motorists are very fortunate in that they have such an excellent aid to non-verbal communication, the Highway Code. Theoretically at least, if we all obeyed this document and remained sober, there would be far fewer road accidents; but of course we don't. In an area such as theatre, where silence is often necessary, signs are a valuable and vital aid to communication, e.g. 'Radium in use', 'Fire exit', 'wet floor'. Statutory Instrument 1980, No. 1471,[6] was prepared by the Health and Safety Commission in conjunction with the British Standards Institution as a result of new regulations governing safety signs in the workplace and came into effect on 1 January 1981. This complies with an EEC directive on the subject issued in 1977. The Instrument gives the employer the opportunity to draw the attention of his employees to a certain course of action by displaying a particular sign, e.g. 'Laser in use'.

Times have changed in hospital life and this is very evident in theatre. We now have a maze of sophisticated equipment, techniques which would not have been thought possible 20 years ago, improved pay and working conditions for nurses, Joint Board courses to produce safe practitioners, and a conglomoration of ancillary workers to relieve the theatre nurse of 'non-nursing' duties. Inherent in this change is the ever-present risk that personal contact with patients and indeed colleagues will be lost. Knowledge is becoming obsolete at a bewildering rate and there is a never-ending race to keep informed of new developments.

It is in this fast-moving world of constant change that theatre nurses have to practise. Despite all the progress which has been made, lack of communication is still often given as the reason mistakes occur. There are many definitions of communication, but in modern jargon it could be defined as 'being on the same wavelength' or 'clued in'. John Donne's 'No man is an island' reminds us that we cannot function alone and theatre staff need to communicate and have good relations with a variety of other people and departments.

It is unlikely that ideal conditions will ever exist for effective communication. We must therefore ensure that infatuation with the science of modern medicine does not blind us to the unchanging needs of our patients: a kind word, a smiling face and compassionate care. Miss Brysson-Whyte, formerly Director of Nurse Education at Guy's Hospital, tells a story about a junior nurse who was told by a very frightening ward sister to go and get something for a patient. The little nurse was amazed by what sister said but was too nervous to question it. She dutifully went to a cupboard and rummaged but couldn't find what she needed. Just then, a more approachable sister came by and asked if she could help. Nurse then explained that sister asked her to get the cod's eyes for Mrs Brown's bed. Putting two and two together, relying on a wealth of experience and without a trace of a smile, sister suggested that perhaps the ward sister really meant 'cot sides'!

We really do have to learn to *listen*, as illustrated by this message sent from the front line during the Second World War: 'Send reinforcements, we're going to advance', which arrived at its destination as: 'Send three and fourpence, we're going to a dance.'

## Summary

No one will dispute that communication in hospital could be improved. Human communication is a complex business but one which we take for granted because we are always involved in it. Making it work is difficult and demands a great deal of thought, time and effort. It would not be realistic to hope that there would be a uniform policy in theatre for passing on information, and therefore the responsibility for this rests with each individual.

Communication errors can be compounded by ignorance, indifference or fear but we are all guilty at times of being obscure. This may be so because we have got into the habit of using convenient abbreviations or technical terms. Nursing is a science and an art which relies heavily on verbal communication and the nurse must be able to communicate effectively and safely with patients and colleagues.

In an age in which everything is being challenged and patients are becoming more assertive about their rights there is a danger that theatre staff may become defensive about passing on information, particularly to patients, because of the possible risk of incrimination. When the ability to communicate at a personal level is not used to its full potential, our contact with patients and each other can regress to a state of nothing more than aloof formality. Strict adherence to agreed procedures can help to avoid many communication errors but, ultimately, responsibility rests with each individual to ensure that communication is effective.

**References**

1. 'The need for flexibility', *Nursing Standard*. Report on Royal College of Nursing International Conference, 1 October 1981.
2. D&C = dilatation and curretage, Ts&As = tonsillectomy and adenoidectomy, ERPC = evacuation of retained products of conception, TAH = total abdominal hysterectomy, BSO = bilateral salpingoopherectomy, EUA = examination under anaesthetic, DPNS = diathermy of post-nasal space, CABG = coronary artery bypass graft, THR = total hip replacement, TUR = transurethral resection.
3. John Field, *News of the World*, 16 December 1979.
4. Steve Valentine, 'Hospital gets wrong op rap', *News of the World*, 22 March 1981.
5. *Yorkshire Evening Post*, 14 October 1982.
6. Statutory Instrument 1980, No. 1471, HMSO.

# 6  THE NURSE'S LIABILITY FOR NEGLIGENCE

For practical purposes, negligence can be regarded as an act or omission not in accordance with the standard of care of a reasonable nurse. To prove negligence, it must first be established that a duty of care was owed to the patient and that there has been a breach of that duty, either by an act of omission, or of commission, resulting in damage being suffered by the person to whom the duty was owing. A 'reasonable' nurse is one who is considered to be well-trained and efficient, acting in accordance with established medical and nursing practices at the time. She is not expected to be a 'super' nurse, and is only expected to act in a given situation according to her level of knowledge, training and experience. It is not enough that her superior can vouch for the fact that she is 'reasonable'; there must be additional recorded information to support this fact. Should a nurse act negligently, excuses such as 'she should know better, she has been here long enough' will not absolve the employing authority for her actions.

Firstly, in order to achieve a satisfactory standard of efficiency, there must be written objectives based on a curriculum for the nurse's training/education. Then a specific time must be determined in which the objectives should be achieved in stages; e.g. at the end of six weeks' experience, she will be skilled in bedmaking/'scrubbing-up'. Initial teaching, observation, guidance and assessment will determine whether or not the objective has been achieved, and so on throughout training.

Take the example of a post-basic student in the operating theatre. Provided she is being taught and shows evidence that she is achieving the appropriate objective, it could be said that at the end of, say, six months she is 'skilled in the care of patients in the anaesthetic room'. If the surgeon is to use diathermy during the operation then one of this nurse's duties will be to apply a diathermy plate to this patient. Should she fail to do this, then she may be said to be negligent in her duty. It cannot be regarded as an accident, it is an omission through carelessness. The extent of damages as a result of this will depend on the result of the omission: e.g. the surgeon may decide not to use diathermy; he

56

may use it, but another member of staff may notice that a diathermy plate is not in position and apply one; the omission may not be noticed and consequently when diathermy is used the patient may suffer a burn; he may suffer considerably post-operatively because of the burn; he may spend longer than was originally necessary in hospital; the burn may contribute to his death. Whether or not a negligence claim applies will depend on the outcome of the above circumstances.

If the absence of a diathermy plate is noticed in time then no harm will come to the patient but the Theatre Sister has a duty to bring the seriousness of the situation to the nurse's attention and caution her of the consequence to herself and her patient even if there are no legal consequences. If the patient suffers physical injury or the omission contributes, in any degree, to his death then the nurse would be held liable for negligence; there has been a breach of the duty of care which this nurse – a trained nurse – owes to her patient and her standard of care has fallen below that of a 'reasonable' nurse. In any ensuing legal proceedings she will be judged according to the standards required of a theatre nurse and not by those of a ward nurse.

One very good reason why all nurses should carry some form of indemnity insurance, either privately or by membership of a professional body or union, is that although employers are held vicariously liable for 'wrong doings' committed by their employees, there is nothing to prevent them making good their own loss — paid in compensation by claiming against the employee.

Cases of retained foreign bodies, e.g. a swab or instrument, have been well publicised, but despite the recommendations of the Medical Defence Union and Royal College of Nursing incidents continue to occur with monotonous regularity. In the past, the 'captain of the ship' doctrine prevailed in operating theatres in the UK; if a foreign body had unintentionally been left in a patient during surgery, it was most unlikely that the 'scrubbed' nurse would be involved in any ensuing legal proceedings; this was the surgeon's responsibility. And despite all that has been said and written by nurses over the years, as theatre nurses we must accept that the surgeon continues to be responsible for the patient's treatment in theatre. However, the shift in the relationship between surgeons and theatre nurses, together with improved education for all nurses, has brought about the concept of teamwork and this in turn means that each member of the team can be held responsible for his/her own actions.

Now, just because a swab has been left in a patient it does not automatically constitute negligence. The patient's condition could have deteriorated during the operation and the surgeon may decide to suture the wound with all due haste, even before there is time to check the swabs. So long as this is recorded in the patient's notes, then there is no cause for alarm. It could also happen that, for some unknown reason, non-radio-opaque swabs are used, and the fact that one is missing may not be recognised until after the incision has been sutured. Obviously, the presence of this swab in the wound cannot be confirmed by X-ray and it may be that the patient is too ill to submit to further surgery at this time to check for the presence of the swab. You may well think that the use of non-radio-opaque swabs is in itself blatant negligence, but there are still theatres in the UK where non-radio-opaque Turkish towels are used as packs during surgery, in preference to X-ray detectable gauze rolls. It seems reasonable to assume that this dangerous practice is sanctioned by the Theatre Procedure Committee and agreed by the hospital authority. So who is to blame when a swab is left in a wound?

**Figure 6.1**: Cases reported to the Medical Defence Union of retained foreign bodies (swabs, instruments, needles, drains and tubes)

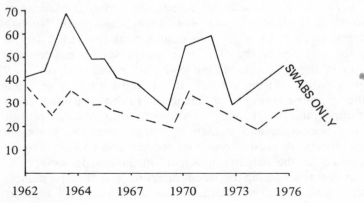

While it is true that the surgeon is responsible for performing the operation, and except in exceptional circumstances for ensuring that swabs are not inadvertently left in a patient, his responsibility ends there. Unless he is told otherwise, he is entitled to be able to trust the theatre staff to provide a safe environment for the patient and this includes adhering to the procedures which are recommended by the Medical Defence Union and Royal College of Nursing. Figure 6.1 speaks for itself.[1]

The practice of cutting the radio-opaque swabs during surgery is a dangerous one and again disregards the recommendations. Performing the wrong operation may again be due to the combined negligence of a number of staff. So many people only want to help and many experienced theatre sisters will have the patient draped even before the surgeon has 'scrubbed'. Because from experience he has learnt to trust the sister, he may well go ahead and operate, only to find when it is too late that it is the wrong patient/side/site or even operation (see Table 6.1). Of course the surgeon should check all this himself and it is becoming increasingly important that he does so. The following case is a typical example.

**Table 6.1:** *Wrong operations*[2]

| Year | Wrong patient or operation | Wrong side | Wrong digit | Total |
|------|----------------------------|------------|-------------|-------|
| 1960 | 1 | 6 | 2 | 9 |
| 1961 | 3 | 12 | 8 | 23 |
| 1962 | 5 | 11 | — | 16 |
| 1963 | 3 | 5 | 5 | 13 |
| 1964 | 2 | 11 | 10 | 23 |
| 1965 | 4 | 11 | 1 | 16 |
| 1966 | 6 | 3 | 2 | 11 |
| 1967 | 5 | 16 | 5 | 26 |
| 1968 | 4 | 7 | 2 | 13 |
| 1969 | 3 | 10 | 3 | 16 |
| 1970 | 6 | 13 | 4 | 23 |
| 1971 | 5 | 8 | 4 | 17 |
| 1972 | 7 | 8 | 7 | 22 |
| 1973 | 8 | 7 | 1 | 16 |
| 1974 | 5 | 9 | 2 | 16 |
| 1975 | 12 | 7 | 3 | 22 |
| 1976 | 5 | 8 | 7 | 20 |

A lady was admitted as a day case for excision of a cyst on her left middle finger . . . the registrar marked the finger and hand. The patient was listed at first, but the order was changed. . . . When the patient came to theatre, the anaesthetist thought she was the patient for carpal tunnel and a tourniquet was applied. A left median nerve decompression was performed but when she was returned to the ward the mistake was recognised. Later, the correct operation was performed. A settlement of £300 was shared equally between the Surgeon's Society and the hospital on behalf of the other staff who were responsible for the mistake over the theatre list.[3]

Some nurses are negligent due to ill health or 'incapacity'. Others are simply negligent. A nurse's qualification entails honouring her committment to uphold a predetermined standard of care and (at the time of writing) if her professional conduct falls below this level her behaviour can be investigated by the General Nursing Council.

'In the year ended March 1981, more than 600 nurses became the subject of investigations by the General Nursing Council . . . to decide if it was appropriate for them to retain the right to practice . . . or whether (in the interest of the public) that right should be withdrawn'.[4] In the two months up to December 1982, 17 nurses were removed from the Register or Roll following 44 cases considered by the General Nursing Council's Disciplinary Committee.[5] 'The United Kingdom Central Council's first disciplinary case to be heard was seen as an historic occasion. It was also the first time that a Health Visitor had been called to answer for her professional misconduct . . . the Central Council for the Education and Training of Health Visitors had no disciplinary function'.[6]

Examples of negligence in theatre are numerous: failing to test equipment before use; not adhering to the procedure for swab, needle and instrument count in *every* case; leaving patients unattended; absence of a teaching programme for new staff, yet allowing them to perform duties for which they have not been trained (in this case it is not the nurse who is negligent but the theatre manager); incorrect labelling of specimens, without double checking; changing the order of the operating list and not informing the appropriate members of staff. The list is endless.

There are many reasons why a theatre nurse should not be negligent and high on this list is the 'duty of care' she owes to her patients. Also, she is subject to the Law, both as an individual and as a professional. And, at a time when unemployment is high in the UK, she would do well to remember her need to work. The recent reports in the press of threatened staff cuts in the National Health Service have now become a reality.

Social Services Secretary Norman Fowler last week in a Commons written reply confirmed earlier press reports that 14 RHAs in England would be asked to cut staff by between 0.75 and 1.00 per cent by next March.[7]

## Summary

The Law does not ask that every operation is successful, but it does demand that the professionals who are charged with the care of the patient are not negligent in the delivery of this care. A theatre nurse is only expected to perform those duties normally expected of her defined functions, and if a situation arises where she is unable or incapable of doing this it is the duty of her manager to ensure that she is not given this responsibility.

Inexperience of staff, a heavy workload, faulty equipment, shortage of staff and general inefficiency are not good enough reasons for delivering patient care which can only be described as dangerous: this is negligence by management for allowing such a situation to arise. Theatre nurses must learn to question what they do not understand and ensure that they are not criticised for action taken which is outside their control.

## References

1. Memoranda of the Medical Defence Union and Royal College of Nursing, 'Safeguards against wrong operations' and 'Safeguards against failure to remove swabs' (1978).
2. Ibid.
3. Medical Protection Society Annual Report and Accounts, 1976, Claims in Negligence (Medical), pp. 40-41.
4. Reginald H. Pyne, *Professional Discipline*, Medical Education (International) Ltd, 1982.

5. 'Latest statistics', *Nursing Standard*, 9 December 1982.
6. 'A professional landmark', *Nursing Standard*, 4 August 1983.
7. 'Staff cuts confirmed', *Nursing Standard*, 4 August 1983.

# 7 ACCIDENTS TO PATIENTS AND STAFF

Twenty years ago, accidents just didn't happen in theatre, or if they did, they were rarely heard about. The whole area was much more insular and theatre staff, like surgeons, were considered an elite group. The normal working week was 48 hours but permanent theatre staff had to be available to 'cover' for night emergencies and weekends; ward staff could not relieve theatre staff; there were no Joint Board courses and in any case, the chronic shortage of nurses in some hospitals made it impossible to increase staffing levels. Staff who settled for theatre work usually remained in it and it was probably the only real speciality in many hospitals. Then, as now, nurse's pay was considered well below the national average and there wasn't any extra pay for the theatre staff who gave a 24 hours a day, seven days a week 'cover'. Despite all these obstacles, theatre nurses struggled on, maintaining very high standards, simply by doing all the work themselves. They were probably only marginally better off than their sixteenth-century counterparts who were often paid in bread and beer.

Then two important events opened the doors of theatre to the rest of the world: the development of Joint Board of Clinical Nursing Studies theatre courses and the introduction of the Nursing Process. After a lifetime of being a 'closed shop', theatre was now under the eagle eye of outsiders. The teaching commitment of trained staff was considerably increased and pre- and post-operative visiting of patients was introduced. After what seemed a lifetime of being able to 'run their own show', theatre staff found themselves accountable to an infinite variety of people: School of Nursing, a Nursing Process Co-ordinator and, above all, a host of eager students asking questions.

It was only to be expected that there would be problems: Procedures had to be reviewed and clarified to meet the learners' needs; trained staff had to update their own knowledge to keep pace with the learners' demands; and the increased sophistication of techniques, and nursing and 'non-nursing' duties, had to be identified and re-allocated. All in all, it was a traumatic time. Whereas in the past, the 'work' was the main priority, now the qualified staff had to teach and monitor the progress of students, relate much more readily to other areas – particularly the surgical wards – and, above all, be 'accountable'. This was a new word in nursing jargon and it took some time for staff to realise exactly what it meant. Previously, theatre staff could turn their hands to anything – fix a fuse, repair equipment, mop the floor and even suture when required – but suddenly it seemed that they were no longer considered competent to do all this. They were expected to 'nurse' and let other experts mend the fuses. This was very difficult for the diehards and indeed to this day there are theatre sisters who have resisted the changes. Be that as it may, there is no doubt that if theatre staff insist on continuing the old regime they can easily be held responsible for accidents which may occur, due to their own incompetence.

The frantic speed at which surgical techniques have developed has made it imperative that staff become familiar with a bewildering variety of new equipment. There was a time when all that was needed for a mastoidectomy was a set of fine orthopaedic instruments; now it requires a microscope: tubal ligation can now be performed through a laprascope, surgical diathermy is in common use, laser is becoming increasingly popular, we have ventilators, monitors, photography image intensifiers and many other pieces of equipment, all of which can cause accidents if handled by staff who are not familiar with their use.

**The Patient**

Long before the patient comes to theatre, preparation will be made by the ward staff to ensure his safety. The ward sister is ultimately responsible for the safety and welfare of her patients and in order to ensure that her staff maintain the required standard all ward procedures must be clearly defined and easy to follow. However, the ratio of learners to trained staff in National Health hospitals is very high and most nursing duties are carried out by learners: Therefore, unless there is a well-defined policy for the supervision and teaching of learners, it is inevitable that accidents will occur.

Patients cannot be expected to be acquainted with the routine preparations for theatre, e.g. if the reason for fasting is not explained to them they may well come to theatre with a full stomach. This is particularly true of children, and anaesthetic tragedies due to this are all too well documented. Therefore, if there is to be continuity of care the patient's treatment and progress must be clearly and legibly documented. Gone are the days when 'ISQ' sufficed as a means of informing staff about a patient's condition. Pre-operative visiting by theatre staff can do much to avoid the danger of accidents occurring due to inadequate information about the patient.

Perhaps the most dangerous situation of all is when the wrong patient is sent to theatre. This of course should never happen but it only takes a particular set of circumstances to allow it to occur all too often. Sister is at lunch, the ward is busy with few nursing staff on duty and the porter arrives from theatre for the first patient but does not ask for him by name. Then a busy nurse indicates the patient's bed and he is duly helped on to the trolley: A student nurse is called to accompany the patient to theatre; she may not know the patient and is simply doing what she's told. However, what the nurse in charge does not know is that the order of the operation list has been changed and the first patient is now third on the list. If she had adhered to the procedure she would have checked the name on the slip brought by the porter with the patient's name band and hospital number. If the same set of circumstances applies in theatre the patient will probably have an operation he does not require while his actual condition remains untreated. If such a case became the subject of Court proceedings the verdict might be one of negligence.

The journey from the ward to the theatre can be fraught with danger if all safety precautions are not strictly adhered to. The patient must be safely positioned on the trolley, ensuring that there is no pressure on nerves or bony prominences. An accident can easily happen when the patient is transferred from the trolley to the operating table if his head is above the edge of the canvas. If at all possible, a tipping trolley should be used and the ward nurse should ensure that the patient is positioned with his head at the correct end of the trolley and that the trolley sides are properly secured. In some circumstances there is something to be said for the American method of securing the patient with straps.

Since some wards may be a considerable distance from theatre, it is essential that the nurse accompanying the patient has a good knowledge of his condition and is able to administer emergency treatment if required. If the patient is being transported by lift and the lift breaks down, the patient will be totally reliant on the nurse. We should give much more thought to the possibility of this happening and consider what might be required for individual patients: oxygen, extra pillows, a vomit bowl, an inhaler for the asthmatic and a suction unit, but above all a nurse who is knowledgeable and confident enough to reassure the patient.

**Arriving in Theatre**

The first requirement for any patient is a pleasant nurse who shows an interest in him as a fellow human being. This will help to make him feel more confident and secure.

The local procedure for patient identification is the most important procedure in theatre. If this is ignored then there is little point in concerning ourselves with any other. However, there is no legal ruling which tells us exactly how this should be done but it should not be beyond the bounds of possibility that we can find out who the patient actually is. Too many nurses are slaves to ritual, ignoring the use of their own intelligence and common sense. Some theatres rely on the use of a checklist and the patient is asked a number of questions to establish his identity. This can be quite frightening for a patient who up to this point may have thought that everyone knew he was going to theatre; he may now wonder if a mistake has already occurred. But whatever means are used, there can be no margin of error. When the patient arrives in the anaesthetic room his identity must be checked by the nurse, the anaesthetist and the surgeon. The side and site of operation should also be checked.

A large number of drugs and anaesthetic agents must be made available in the anaesthetic room. If we are to avoid accidents in their use, there must be a strict code of practice which is applicable to nursing and medical staff. In the UK, it is a legal requirement that the anaesthetist is a doctor, this qualification giving him the right to prescribe and administer drugs; therefore it is his responsibility, and his alone, to mix, draw up and administer the required drugs to the patient in the anaesthetic room. However, a most dangerous practice is slowly but surely creeping into use in some hospitals: the drugs are drawn up and labelled, ready for the list, even before the patient or anaesthetist arrives. This is usually done by non-medical staff in the well-meaning but misguided belief that it is an efficient means of saving time. Pre-printed labels, e.g. 'contaminated material' or 'not for intravenous use', are a reliable means of identification in many hospital situations, but the practice of leaving labelled loaded syringes ready for use in the anaesthetic room is to be deplored. Have we really become so indifferent to the patient's safety that we take this dangerous and unnecessry risk? Apart from showing a distinct lack of any professional ethics it is a direct contravention of the Medicines Act 1968, which certainly does not authorise either nurses or ODAs to dispense or label drugs and containers. Is there a written policy in your hospital stating that the employing authority sanctions this procedure?

A number of anaesthetic accidents which have occurred in recent years have been widely publicised and there can be little doubt that the more people who are involved in the administration of an anaesthetic, the greater the risk of accident.

The risk of controlled drugs abuse in operating theatres 'could be thought to be greater' than elsewhere in hospital because of the 'comparative ease of access by a number of "anonymous" people in theatre dress'. This is one of the points raised by the Royal College of Nursing in reaction to a report by the Association of Anaesthetists of Great Britain and Ireland on the use of controlled drugs in theatre. In its conclusion the report states 'Recognition by both nurses and anaesthetists that administration is the responsibility of the latter group and accurate record keeping the responsibility of both, should ensure that these drugs be used safely without danger or loss'.[1]

Anaesthetic accidents can also occur when the patient's denture has not been removed and this goes unnoticed in the anaesthetic room.

Confusion continues to exist with regard to the role of the nurse and the operating department assistant in the anaesthetic room. Who does what and where is the dividing line between nursing and technical care? What are the nurses doing when they are not in the anaesthetic room? Perhaps washing and packing instruments? But then many hospitals now have non-nursing staff to do this. Is all their time taken up teaching the continuous stream of new learners now invading theatre – student nurses arriving every three weeks and maybe post-basic students twice a year? They can't be doing all the 'managing' because that is the responsibility of Nursing Officers and the Senior Nursing Officer. Maybe the answer lies in the fact that theatre nurses have taken on too much responsibility in the past with little or no consideration of their own personal or professional rights. They were conditioned into accepting submissive and dependent roles; now the ODAs have clearly defined job descriptions and there is an urgent need to have the role and responsibilities of the theatre nurse equally clearly defined. If nursing is supposed to be about caring for the sick then it must follow that wherever there is a patient there must also be a nurse. If the patient in the anaesthetic room, or indeed in any area of the operating theatre, has an accident due to the absence of nursing care then the responsibility rests with the Nurse Manager.

Hospital authorities have a legal and moral responsibility to maintain certain quality standards in all aspects of patient care and theatre nurses, as employees, must ensure that this responsibility is honoured in their department.

**Lasers**

Now more than ever before the opportunities for accidents occurring are limitless, especially with the increasing use of lasers. The story is told of a firm's representative who was demonstrating laser equipment to a surgeon over coffee. While he listed the many benefits of this miracle gadget, he hadn't noticed that he had inadvertently burned some enormous holes in his briefcase. A lesson perhaps in what can happen when new equipment is used by the untrained. The Department of Health and Social Security has issued draft national guidelines on laser safety in medical practice. This important document[2] outlines health authorities' duties in providing safe organisational arrangements and encourages employers to formulate local rules for the protection of patients and staff. Lasers can cause blindness if not used properly and all theatre staff involved in the use of this potentially lethal equipment should be fully conversant with its hazards and the means whereby accidents can be avoided.

# Fire

The risk of fire occurring in the operating theatre is very high and this risk is increased if staff are not knowledgeable in recognising risks where they exist and of taking effective action to minimise them. The Health and Safety at Work Act 1974 applies to all premises where people are at work and the Fire Precautions Act 1971 requires that Crown premises, i.e. National Health hospitals, have a Fire Certificate, which is issued by the Fire Service inspectorate of the Home Office. Applying these Acts to the operating theatre department means in effect that provision must be made for:

an effective fire alarm system; the provision of firefighting equipment; an effective means of escape for patients and staff; the maintenance of fire-resistant doors; the appointment of a Fire Officer within the department, who will be responsible for ensuring that: all staff are familiar with the equipment and its use, arrangements are made to hold fire drills and simulated evacuation exercises, and all fire exits are kept clear and free from obstruction and that appropriate locking devices are functioning.

Above all, the department Fire Officer, in conjunction with the Hospital Fire Prevention Officer, should ensure by continuing education that each member of theatre staff has sufficient knowledge to deal with an outbreak of fire, avoiding as far as possible accidents to both patients and colleagues.

Faulty equipment is a potential fire hazard and under no circumstances should nurses attempt to effect repairs. This equipment should be repaired by the appropriate hospital department or in certain cases, arrangements may exist whereby it is repaired by the manufacturer.

# Electrosurgery

Electrosurgery is an advancement which is now in common use but one which has been responsible for a number of accidents, usually because of the lack of knowledge of theatre staff. We must all have encountered situations where the surgeon asked to have the diathermy setting increased and someone helpfully does so. If it didn't work on that setting, it was turned up again and so on until someone decided that perhaps something was wrong. Fortunately in most cases no harm came to the patient and once the fault was identified and corrected, the equipment worked satisfactorily. However, we cannot always rely on luck and simply by adhering to a few basic simple rules, many accidents could be avoided. Ensure that there is a standing arrangement with manufacturers for regular checking and servicing of machines and routine inspection by theatre staff each time the equipment is going to be used. Electrosurgery can ignite flammable or explosive anaesthetics, so check with the anaesthetist as to the type of anaesthetic agent to be used. Make sure that the patient is not in direct or indirect contact with exposed metal.

Check in advance if the patient has an implanted cardiac pacemaker. The manufacturer will be able to give information regarding possible interference problems. Be aware that monitoring electrodes may cause electrical interference.


## Sharps Disposal

Sharps of one type or another are used in most operations, such as suture needles, scalpel blades, hypodermic needles, skin graft blades and glass ampoules. Their disposal in the past has been a fairly 'hit and miss' affair and every nurse new to theatre was expected to have at least one accident with sharps. It was almost an established ritual; once the sharps were removed from the trolley at the end of a case and placed in a bag or bin, their disposal was someone else's concern. But this situation no longer applies. The Health and Safety Act provides for 'the health, safety and welfare of people at work', and this means everyone, including the nurse who 'scrubs' the staff in the anaesthetic room and the porters who remove the rubbish. There must be a safe and reliable means whereby sharps are disposed of and whichever method is used, it must conform to the standards required by the Control of Infection policy. Collecting all the sharps used in any one day in a large plastic container is certainly not the answer. This can be a source of infection, or unnecessary hazard.

**Staff Protection**

Quite rightly we pay considerable attention to protecting our patients from accidents, but the employing authority has a legal duty to ensure that staff are also protected. National Health hospitals are not subject to the Employers Liability (Compulsory Insurance) Act 1969 so a health authority held liable to pay damages, in the case of an accident to a member of staff, will have to find the money from its own budget.

> At the conclusion of an operation carrying poles were passed through the side channels of the canvas on which the patient was lying. The anaesthetist then lifted the poles at the head end and a theatre nurse lifted at the foot end, whereupon the patient slid between the operating table and the trolley, falling to the floor . . . there was already a canvas stretcher on the table when the patient was lifted on to the operating table. One pole had been placed into this cover and the other into the cover on which the patient lay. . .[3]

This patient suffered from various complications post operatively: double vision for which an exploratory operation was carried out, showing adherence of the right medial rectus muscle to the medial wall of the orbut, which had been fractured during the original operation – an intra-nasal polypectomy.

> A muscle transplant was performed to improve adduction when the insertion of the superior and inferior recti were moved to positions adjacent to the insertion of the medial rectus muscle. Later, a right and left lateral rectus recession operation was performed to overcome the divergent deviation . . . the patient still had double vision on looking to the left . . . also some facial disfigurement.[3]

The claim was settled for £5,000 plus costs.


**Economy**

At a time when every penny spent within the National Health Service must be accounted for, there needs to be concrete evidence that the present expenditure is justified. Indeed, as long ago as 1979 the following statement appeared:

A reduction of one third in the number of theatre nurses in the United Kingdom to 8,000 and a 100% increase in the number of Operating Department Assistants to 6,000 would show a cost benefit of £66.6 million, and offer hospitalisation to a further 240,000 patient per year.[4]

If theatre nurses wish to be involved in the broader aspects of patient care they will need to establish their own parameters of care and avoid becoming complacent. The National Association of Theatre Nurses' Codes of Practice recommends 'the minimal level below which no standard should fall' and this valuable document outlines practices which should be followed to avoid accidents to staff and patients in the operating theatre.

## Summary

Accidents should never happen and when they do the result is often unnecessary pain and suffering. The increased use of electrical equipment in theatre work automatically increases the risk of accidents but this can be avoided if staff are knowledgeable and vigilant. There is now sufficient legislation to determine standards of care; however, legislation does not, by itself, ensure that standards are upheld but it does impose sanctions if it is not complied with. The ultimate responsibility for safe practice will always rest with the individual. Deficiency in administration and a lowering of standards of care can contribute to tragic consequences for which there is now adequate machinery for patients to seek redress.

## References

1. 'College critical of report on use of controlled drugs', *Nursing Standard*, 12 August 1982.
2. *Guidelines on Laser Safety*, DHSS, 1983.
3. *Annual Report and Accounts*, Medical Protection Society, 1976, p. 36.
4. *Technic*, April 1979.

# 8 RECORD-KEEPING

Time was when the most important records kept on the ward were the report and the intake and output charts. There was a fairly well-established routine for writing the report:

Slept well
No change
Little to report
ISQ
Restless at times otherwise nothing to report
Comfortable day/night
Seems rather withdrawn otherwise nothing to report
C/o pain 12 mn. Aspirin 10 mgms given. Slept well afterwards
Good night/day

The busy night nurse, frequently looking after a ward of 30 patients on her own, would often bracket together the 'no change' patients. For the patient who had been to theatre, a more detailed report would be written, e.g. 'returned from theatre 4 p.m. Regained consciousness 6 p.m. Pethidine 50 mgms given 6.30 p.m. Continue I.V. 20 drops per minute. Nil by mouth. Restless at times.'

*Collin's English Dictionary* defines 'report' as 'give an account of'. Just how much information staff could elicit from the kind of report outlined above we will never know but the format was used in hospitals throughout the UK; indeed the belief was the less one wrote, the better. Some night nurses were known to write the night report at 4 a.m. before they started the morning work. The day report was written by sister and if she was due to go off duty at 9 p.m. she would start the report about 7 p.m., writing only about the patients who were reasonably well and leaving the very ill ones until later. Report writing was seen as a senior responsibility but for many staff-nurses on busy wards it was probably the only time they sat down.

The intake and output charts were the pride and joy of many ward sisters and were considered works of art. Not all nurses were allowed to fill them in, using coloured ink. The nurses would use pencil and at the end of the day sister would complete them, using red and green ink. When temperature charts were introduced the patient's temperatures were entered in a book and again sister would fill in the charts. However, it must be said that although the written report gave little real information about any patient, sister made it her business to know all there was to know about each individual patient and it was enough that nurses carried out her orders. So why are reports considered so important now? Quite simply because they are regarded with greater importance for the protection of both patients and staff. A report should convey specific information, it must be clearly written and factual. 'A nursing report should contain all the information that a nurse, new to the care of the patient, needs to know in order to continue that care and to assess whether such care is effective'.[1]

Before the introduction of the new legislation, the most important record in theatre was the operation register, and this too was filled in by sister at the end of the day. This practice went on for years and there is no doubt that every entry was accurate.

Historically, nurses have focused on their duties, and the task of record-keeping was considered the responsibility of managers. However, although all documentation may not start out as a legal document it can easily become one. A case may not come to Court for years but if it does then all documentation relating to the patient will become evidence. The recollections of the staff involved may have faded and become less reliable with the passage of time and the records may be the only real evidence available. One of the most controversial pieces of legislation proposed in Britain for decades was the Police and Criminal Evidence Bill which proposed that the police should be given power to apply for a judge's ruling as to whether medical records of a suspect should be made available during preliminary investigations. However, in April 1983 the government climbed down and the Home Secretary agreed that police could not demand the records.[2]

Paperwork in nursing has increased considerably and is often seen by nurses as an unnecessary chore; consequently little attention is paid to what is written. The practice of the Nursing Process is a good example; either too much attention is paid to the recording, to the detriment of the patient, or little or nothing is written. Good record-keeping is an integral part of nursing care and it is also a means of self-protection for the nurse. Terminology is an important element in the writing of records; what may seem like a humorous comment when it is written may become a defamatory statement when read out in Court.

Here are just some of the records which may be used in hospital:

*The patient*:

*Doctors*: Outpatient notes, history, findings on examination, investigation reports.

*Ward Nurses*: Nursing Process records, urinalysis, TPR, intake and output charts, temperature, pulse and respiration, Kardex, ward report.

*Theatre*: Operation list, operating register, drug register, policies, procedures, accident forms for staff and patients, consent forms, swab, needle and instrument count record, operation notes, anaesthetic notes, recovery notes.

*All nursing staff*: Objectives, assessments, job descriptions, contracts, appraisal, discontinuation policy, district and hospital policies, (e.g. fire, health and safety), warning notices, minutes, orders, references, information on staff convicted under the Rehabilitation of Offenders Act 1974, DHSS and District circulars.

Some or all of those records may be used. The information they contain must be objective, factual and legible. Abbreviations must not be used and if an incorrect entry is made a line should be drawn through this and a brief explanation written. Tippex or erasers must never be used. Records should be kept in a secure place and should only be available to the appropriate staff.

## Patients' Records

All changes in a patient's treatment or condition must be entered in the appropriate record and entries made by nursing staff must carry a full signature. In order that records are properly kept, instruction in the methods used should be given to all staff. This is particularly important in the case of agency staff who may not be familiar with the methods used in the particular hospital. It hardly needs to be said that an entry regarding treatment should not be made in the record until the treatment has actually been carried out and all entries must be made in indelible ink.

## Staff Records

A variety of forms are used to record the nurse's achievement, behaviour and professional development, from the beginning of training and throughout her professional career. This is the only formal means whereby the employing authority can monitor progress and ensure that the required standards are being maintained. If for any reason this is not being done, and a situation arises where a nurse's standard of patient care or her general behaviour falls below an acceptable level, then in ordinary circumstances her employer would have difficulty in dismissing her. Her defence could be that she had not been told the terms of her employment and the standard of patient care required, and that under these circumstances she was doing the best she could. This situation applies particularly in the case of a student or pupil nurse.

An employer must be able to show that he acted fairly and support his reasons for dismissing any employee. And according to the Trade Unions and Labour Relations Act, if he cannot show just cause for so doing he can be called before an industrial tribunal and possibly sued by the employee for unfair dismissal.

## Confidentiality and Disclosure of Information

Contrary to popular belief, doctors and nurses do not have an automatic legal privilege for non-disclosure of information; however, this is not to say that we should misuse the trust our patients have in us, as professional people. The Royal College of Nursing has issued guidelines for nurses explaining the nurses' responsibility in regard to confidentiality. This stresses the importance of maintaining the bond of trust between patient and nurse and makes it clear that confidentially is not a legal requirement but a matter of professionalism.

Paragraph 1.2 of the guidelines states 'except where required by law of the country concerned, a nurse shall not disclose without the consent of the patient, information which is obtained in the course of her professional relationship with the patient.' Rule (a), paragraph 1.3, states 'A nurse being in a fiduciary capacity, that is to say, a position of trust, must preserve the patient's confidences unless relieved from this obligation by some lawful excuse.' Lawful excuse can be interpreted as appearance in Court as a witness in criminal or civil proceedings relating to the patient.[3] In this situation, the nurse must behave as any other lawabiding citizen, telling the truth, the whole truth and nothing but the truth.

Other instances where it would seem sensible for a nurse to pass on information given to her in confidence by a patient would be:

1. The patient tells her that he has saved all his sleeping tablets and plans to take an overdose.
2. He tells her that he intends injuring another patient or a member of staff.
3. He intimates that the history he gave to the doctor was in fact false.
4. A patient arrives in theatre for surgery and tells the nurse that he has had a recent meal, but doesn't want the anaesthetist to know.
5. The same patient tells the theatre nurse that he is a drug addict.
6. A patient coming to theatre for evacuation of retained products of conception explains to the nurse that this is a result of an illegal abortion, but that she hasn't given this information to the surgeon.

There is no doubt that some confidences are better divulged, in the interest of the patient and in some cases for the safety and welfare of other patients and staff. For the nurse who is unsure and who may feel that it would be unethical to repeat information given to her in confidence, her wisest choice is to seek the advice of the sister in charge, who may decide that the situation is sufficiently serious to consult with the doctor. A nurse owes 'a duty of care' not just to one patient but to all patients and she also owes a duty to her colleagues. The patient's treatment is the combined responsibility of the doctor and nurses and this treatment cannot be effective if all relevant information is not available to them.

## Giving of Information to the Press

You may just have 'scrubbed' for the first successful brain transplant in the country, but you do not have the right to inform all the newspapers of this fact! A hospital spokesman is appointed to liaise with the press and television and he will have a carefully prepared statement for them. The surgeon who performed the operation may make a statement to the press and be interviewed on TV but, if you are invited to do either, you must first have the permission of your employer. The nearest you might get to stardom is seeing yourself on TV if the hospital authorities have given permission for the operation to be filmed. When transplantations were first performed, reporters were understandably to be seen hovering around hospitals waiting to get a 'scoop'. However, it cannot be overemphasised that nurses must be ever-vigilant regarding conversations about their work. I was once telephoned by the editor of a nursing journal for a 'chat'. During the course of this 'chat' he asked about facilities in teaching as opposed to non-teaching hospitals. Quite innocently, I said that hospitals 'in the sticks' had fewer facilities than those in the city. Some weeks later I read an article in the journal headed 'London nurse says hospitals in the "sticks" are not well off'! I had lots of letters from nurses asking me who gave me the right to criticise their hospital!

## Giving of Information to Patients and Relatives

Particular care should be exercised over the disclosure of information by nurses to relatives. Confidential information should not be disclosed, unless the nurse is already aware that the patient has given permission; even then it is the doctor's duty to inform the relatives of the situation in the first place. The doctor will also be the person to give the patient information about his condition, treatment and prognosis. This will then be reinforced by the nursing staff, and this procedure highlights the importance of effective communication between doctors and nurses. Breakdown in this line of communication can have disastrous results, as shown by the following example.

A young woman was admitted for biopsy of a breast lump. After surgery she was returned to the ward to await the result of the biopsy. The situation had been clearly explained to her by the surgeon beforehand and she naturally hoped that the lump would be benign. Two days after the operation, she hadn't heard from the surgeon and was beginning to feel quite hopeful. Her hopes were soon dashed when a theatre nurse came to visit her, explaining that she would be looking after her when she came to theatre the next day for a mastectomy. The only problem was that the patient was the one person who did not know about the operation. It can easily happen.

## Disclosure of Information Regarding Staff

The Rehabilitation of Offenders Act 1974 is an Act 'to rehabilitate offenders who have not been reconvicted of any serious offences for periods of years, to penalise the unauthorised disclosure of their previous convictions, to amend the law of defamation and for purposes connected therewith'. However, employers have a legal duty to disclose known convictions under this Act when supplying references for employees, even when the conviction is 'spent'. A nurse who fails to disclose a criminal conviction would also be subject to dismissal under the Act.

## Retention of Records

The Department of Health and Social Security issued a health circular stating the new minimum periods of retention for personal health records (for possible use in litigation) 'to take account of the provisions of the Limitation Act 1975 and the Congenital Disabilities (Civil Liability) Act 1976'. The following information is quoted from the circular.

### *Time Limits of Actions for Personal Injuries*

1. A child born disabled, as distinct from his mother, can bring civil action for damages in respect of that disability, the limitation period being 3 years, but this now runs from when it was realised that a person has suffered a significant injury that may be attributable to the negligence of a third party. For a minor, the limitation period is from the time he attains 18 years and may be extended where material facts are not known.

2. A person of 'unsound mind' can, as long as he remains under the disability in question, bring an action without limit of time through his 'next friend'. After the person's death, the period of limitation will run against his personal representative(s) . . . discharge from hospital can no longer be regarded as implying that the person has ceased to suffer from the disability.

3. The limitation period of 3 years applies only to actions which include a claim for damages in respect of personal injuries. . . .

## Time Limits of Retention of Records

Obstetric records – 25 years.

Children and young people – until the patient's 25th birthday or 8 years after the last entry if longer.

Mentally disordered patients – 20 years from the date when the doctor decides that the disorder has ceased or diminished.

Except that such records need only be retained for a minimum of 8 years after the death of a patient (or in the case of obstetric records, death of a child – but NOT of the mother).

All other personal health records – 8 years after the conclusion of treatment.[4]

## The Police and Criminal Evidence Bill

Some of the proposals of this Bill threatened the future confidentiality of patients' medical records and the longstanding tradition that such records remain confidential. Up to now, only a Court order could force medical staff to disclose information regarding patients, but only to the Court. Clause 10 of the Bill would have extended the Court's power to the police. Considerable pressure was brought to bear to have this clause amended and the then Home Secretary, Mr Whitelaw, announced in a written parliamentary reply that 'confidential personal records kept by the caring and other professions would be exempt from scrutiny'.[5]

## Computers

A number of alternative types of computers are now available for record-keeping. Most computers in use today are digital and store and manipulate entities represented by digits. Some nurses may see computers as monsters of science fiction that could take over nursing completely, but computerised systems of record-keeping are efficient, require far less space and allow quick and easy access to data. With the increase in the amount and importance of records, there is undoubtedly a need for a streamlined system for retaining these records and the development of computers provides the answer.

Computer technology impinges more and more on our daily lives and we accept their influence almost unnoticed: clocks, watches, children's games, and that often unwelcome bank statement. The fear of these technological giants can easily be overcome, even with only a basic knowledge of how they operate, and there is already a need to include teaching of computer appreciation in basic nurse training. For the theatre nurse, the possibilities for the use of a computer are endless – e.g. documentation of the surgical procedure, swab and instrument counts, ordering stocks and supplies, and also as a means of keeping records of current teaching on policies and procedures – thus allowing much more time for nursing. While the completion of records would continue to be the responsibility of the individual nurse, time would be saved and this could ultimately prove to be cost effective.

There has been considerable concern about the possibility of computer information getting into the 'wrong hands', but through the use of access codes, information entry and retrieval can be limited to designated staff only. The Data Protection Bill 1982 applies to automatically processed records, and 'is expedient legislation for Britain to ratify the European Convention for the Protection of Individuals with regard to Automatic Processing of Personal Data'.[6] There are many concerns about this Bill, which could alter the individual's right to freedom and the nurse's role in confidentiality.

## Summary

The *New English Dictionary* defines record as: 'to set down permanent evidence – to imprint deeply on the mind'. While there has always been a certain amount of linguistic free trade among nurses and doctors, it would be unwise to extend this to the written word. Nursing records are changing rapidly and assuming increasing importance. A number of the mishaps that befall patients can be attributed to poor written communication but this is no defence against complaints about errors in patient care.

No law in the book can, by itself, improve the situation: you cannot legislate for attitudes. And although the quality of documentation can establish a valid defence to claims against medical and nursing staff, this should not be our prime reason for good notemaking. We are professionally responsible for the care and safety of our patients and every nurse should be aware that good documentation contributes to this care.

With threats to the safeguards of personal confidences, we as nurses must ensure that we can safely continue to honour the trust of out patients. But we must also recognise that although the rights of the individual to privacy are extremely important, there are occasions when both legally and ethically this privacy cannot be afforded.

## References

1. Royal College of Nursing of the United Kingdom, Association of Nursing Practice, Nursing Records, 23 March 1978.
2. 'Files are safe', *Nursing Standard*, 21 April 1983.
3. *Guidelines on Confidentiality in Nursing*, Royal College of Nursing.
4. 'Health Service Management. Retention of personal health records (for possible use in litigation)', DHSS circular HC (80)7, May 1980.
5. 'Confidentiality controversy', *Nursing Standard*, 21 April 1983.
6. Data Protection Bill, HMSO, 1982.

# 9 TERMINAL ILLNESS AND ISSUE OF THE DYING PATIENT

Please sir, don't force me to live
when my body is ready to die,
It's been so long, and hurt so much,
I've no more tears to cry.

My soul is weary and longs to be free,
but it's trapped in the tube of that constant IV

If I could speak I'd beg of you,
stop the machines, stop the 02,
just ease the pain and let me be,
let me die with dignity.

You mean well, sir, and I thank you for trying
but for me, the living is worse than the dying.
Please, sir, I'm no longer afraid,
I've now accepted my fate,
with comfort and love He waits for me
and you, sir are making me late.[1]

Before the advent of modern medicine, death was not an option. The lucky ones lived their three score years and ten, and any extra time was a bonus. Even today 'natural' death is much more readily accepted by the older generation, and in our enlightened technological age there are still patients for whom modern medicine only prolongs a suffering that in an earlier era would have come to a speedy end.

So what do we understand by 'terminal'? *Nuttall's Everyday Dictionary* defines it as 'the extremity or end' but 'terminate' is defined as 'to put an end to, to finish'. Results of the undoubted progress which has been made in medicine now puts doctors and nurses in a position where they can be responsible for 'putting an end' to a life. Their overriding aim is saving life and curing sickness, but there will inevitably be times when this is not possible. The patient in theatre who has got obvious secondary deposits of carcinoma: is it worthwhile performing extensive surgery, knowing the undoubted risk, in an effort to offer him the possibility of a longer life, despite its quality, or is it more humane to 'sew him up'? The intensive care patient who can only exist on a respirator, when all tests show that there is irreperable brain damage, or the renal patient for whom dialysis is not acceptable and a suitable kidney donor cannot be found – these are just some examples of the dilemmas which have to be faced.

There is considerable uneasiness among nurses who are often ill-prepared to deal with these problems and if there was more extensive teaching on these ethical issues in basic training then perhaps there would be less argument for euthanasia. In *A General Textbook of Nursing* by Evelyn Pearce, first published in 1937,[2] the last chapter is appropriately headed 'The Nursing of the Dying and Care of the Dead' and it outlines the duties of the doctor and the nurse when caring for a dying patient and his relatives. How many modern textbooks do the same?

The Royal College of Nursing has set up a forum for nurses working in hospices, continuing care units and pain control units to help them to share and deepen their knowledge of symptom control and the care of the dying.[3] This is certainly a step in the right direction but should not this be extended to all nurses who inevitably will have to care for the dying? Even the most junior nurse may be involved in caring for a patient whose notes clearly state 'do not resuscitate'; what impression will this make on her if she is unprepared?

Doctors make life or death decisions regularly; they have to, as an integral part of their professional practice, and fortunately the law does not intrude on these decisions; they must always rest with the professional. The nurse, on the other hand, rarely makes decisions, but she will quite often be the person who has to perform the final act that will hasten death. If she is expected to behave as an intelligent member of a profession, it is essential that she is involved in any discussion where the possible outcome may involve her. The nursing profession has to maintain its credibility; nurses must be accountable for their actions and it therefore seems logical to say that no nurse should carry out any action or order against her better judgement. However, this statement must be interpreted in relation to the nurse's level of knowledge and her status.

The student nurse gains her experience and perfects her skills at the bedside and during training there will be many occasions when she is instructed to perform tasks which she finds distasteful or even considers not in the patient's best interest. She has, of course, every right to discuss her concern with sister, but she is rarely in a position where she can object. Sister, however, has every right to discuss patient's treatment with the doctor and it is only by doing this that she can intelligently discuss the patient's progress with staff and relatives.

It is inevitable that nurses working in specialised units e.g. theatre, intensive care and renal, will be involved in ethical decision-making. The practice of the Nursing Process brings to the theatre nurse all relevant information pertinent to each individual patient. She cannot ignore this information and by virtue of preparing for the patient's operation she is involved in his treatment even before he actually comes to theatre. Take the case of an 80-year-old man who has previously had a hemi-mandibulectomy. He is now admitted for further surgery because of extensive secondary deposits. The patient has obviously agreed to submit to this surgery and the decision to operate will have been made by the surgeon, only after careful deliberation. Is there any theatre nurse who can honestly say that she does not, at least in her mind, question the ultimate value of yet further mutilation for this poor man, the ethics of the surgeon's decision, and the psychological effect of the outcome on the patient and his relatives?

If only there was more discussion between the team, anaesthetists, surgeons and theatre nurses – and indeed ward staff too – when decisions such as these are made. Then the nursing staff would have the opportunity to voice their concerns. Very often of course, the nurses themselves are to blame. Some are frightened that if they do speak out they will rock the boat; some are quite happy to accept whatever the doctor decides; and worse still, some just remain silent in the mistaken belief that this is the 'professional' thing to do. Yet time and time again we hear the cry from nurses that they want to be treated as professionals. Perhaps if they acted professionally, their opinions would be treated seriously. Expressions of disagreement may be inconvenient but if there is to be a healthy approach to teamwork, professionals should have a genuine understanding of each other's point of view.

Terminally ill patients who are given modern surgical treatment may live longer, but they will require skilled nursing care, the treatment will be expensive – a very real consideration in the present financial climate – and yet they will probably die surrounded by a maze of equipment instead of a loving family. The issue of consent is of equal importance when deciding on palliative treatment for the dying patient, and for the conscious patient his informed consent must be obtained before any further surgery is arranged. If the patient is unconscious, the proposed surgery should be discussed with the next of kin. However, the question will always remain: should life be preserved at all costs? Contrary to popular belief, Christian churches believe that all efforts to preserve life should only be made by *ordinary*, not *extraordinary*, means, and above all the dignity and sanctity of life should be respected.

'The jury rejected a charge of attempted murder against Doctor Leonard Arthur, on Thursday 5 November 1981 and he walked from the court a free man. They also formally cleared him of murdering the three-day-old boy, unwanted mongol baby John Pearson, after Judge Farquharson ordered the original charge to be dropped.'[4] This case highlighted the dilemma with which doctors are faced and is in contrast to a case, reported earlier in 1981, in which the anguished parents of a ten-day-old mongol baby pleaded that she should not have a life-saving operation and a High Court judge agreed with them; but just three hours later two Appeal Court judges overturned this decision and ruled that the baby must live. After the refusal of the parents, doctors referred the case to a Social Services department and the Council were granted an emergency order over the baby.[5] It is interesting to note that this little baby was transferred from the maternity hospital, where she was born, to another hospital for her surgery, where doctors refused to operate without the parents' consent; she was subsequently transferred to another hospital where doctors referred the case to the Social Services department.

Professional feelings ran high after the Down's baby case; David Rye, Director of Professional Activities of the Royal College of Nursing, said in referring to the case

The position of the nurse is straightforward, she is there to provide nursing care and to carry it out. The only problems arise where there is conflict with the treatment model between nurse and doctor. There has to be, in professional terms, discussions between the professions concerned.

He was opposed to legislation, because it cannot provide decisions in the grey areas, but said the Royal College would issue guidelines on the matter if members wanted them.[6]

So the dilemma continues: when to go to extraordinary lengths to save life and when to allow a patient to die if ordinary treatment is ineffective. The problem is a complex one; proper account must be taken of advances in medical science and technology and what would have been considered impossible a century ago, e.g. kidney transplantation, has now become quite ordinary, yet initially, the operation was 'high risk' and many patients died. Controversy will continue to surround any new and untried surgical procedure and there is no doubt that many procedures will pose moral and ethical problems.

As nurses, we tend to think of the terminally ill patient as one for whom no cure is yet available. Think of the TB patients of long ago; many died in their early youth, despite having the most modern treatment of their time; yet were it not for the continuation of the early pioneering work in research, they would still die today. When it comes to decision-making, nurses can never be equal to doctors and any effort to bring this about would be counter-productive. This, of course, is not to say that they should slavishly obey orders; they must think before they act and be fully aware of the consequences of their actions. They cannot hope to be absolved simply by saying they were obeying orders. At the Nuremberg trials many of the accused offered a plea of mitigation that they were only obeying orders when they helped to send six million Jews to the gas chambers. The world was horrified, particularly when they heard of the health experiments conducted at the concentration camps by doctors, assisted by nurses. Not one nurse was prosecuted at the trials; perhaps it would be a different situation if it happened today.

The ward nurse may often be faced with the problem of interpreting doctor's notes which read 'nursing care only'. Does this mean 'nil by mouth' or does the administration of sustenance rank as a nursing duty? As nurses, we know that the body needs nourishment and if a patient is too ill to be fed orally this can be done intravenously, which could be interpreted as the doctor's duty; but now we are splitting hairs. We can also unravel this instruction and read the unwritten words 'please allow this patient to die painlessly and with dignity'. This may be the most humane way of treating the patient but it is essential that the nurse is aware of the decision which has been made. For many patients, death is not the end and in order to understand their attitude to death we must know something of their philosophy of life. The fear of pain is very often greater than any fear of death, which may be welcomed as a friend. For those who believe in an afterlife, death is but the gateway to an immortal life with their Maker. So why is death seen as a failure of treatment by so many nurses and doctors? After all, we know for sure that it is inevitable yet in some cases we plod on trying one treatment after another, perhaps hoping for a miracle.

Many patients believe in miracles and there are some well-documented cases where despite the doctor's prognosis being negative, the patient actually got better. So how can we ever be sure that decisions made about the patient who seems to be 'terminal' are the right ones? We can't; we can only hope that whatever decision is made will be in the patient's best interest.

In 1600, Shakespeare so clearly described the progression of life in *As You Like It*, from the mewling and puking infant in the nurse's arms to the 'last scene of all/That ends this strange eventful history . . . second childishness and mere oblivion,/sans teeth, sans eyes, sans taste, sans everything.' Birth is anticipated as a joyful happening and what can be more satisfying for the theatre nurse than to assist at a Caesarean birth where a normal healthy baby is delivered? Why is it then that we cannot as readily accept death? After all, it is only the completion of the life process.

Euthanasia has been much discussed in recent years and we now have a Voluntary Euthanasia Society whose aim is to have legalised the right to die with dignity. What, one wonders, is happening to society if we have to invoke the power of the Law to give us this right. Compassion is commendable, but if we surrender to every compassionate impulse we could well open the floodgates and this could eventually be translated into a holocaust. Where would we start? Abort all malformed and/or possibly mentally retarded unborn babies; allow the young chronically ill to die; clear the geriatric wards in one fell swoop; then perhaps start on all patients suffering from a condition for which a cure has not, as yet, been found? Would we next have an age limit at which people must be prepared to die if they could no longer usefully contribute to the national economy and were becoming a burden on the state? The possibilities are endless. As

George Bernard Shaw has said: 'We must not stay as we are, doing always what was done last time, or we shall stick in the mud. Yet neither must we undertake a new world as catastrophic Utopians, and wreck our civilisation in our hurry to mend it.'

Euthanasia can be defined as the painless inducement of death and if it is voluntary, it is induced with the consent of the victim. Whatever the possible benefits of this, it is contrary to Christian teaching which says life is not ours to dispose of and belongs to God; it is against the common good, but more importantly, from a practical viewpoint, it is illegal.

Some people may make prior arrangements about the way in which they wish to die should they be found to have a terminal illness. This might take the form of a private arrangement within a family and although any member of the family involved could be termed an accessory to suicide or murder, judges have been known to show mercy to relatives in this situation, depending, of course, on the circumstances of the individual case.

Jean Humphry knew she was dying of cancer. The 42 year-old mother of three knew the end was near – knew the disease had spread through her spine and was about to enter her brain. Dreading a slow, painful death in a hospital ward, she asked her husband to help her commit suicide under a pact they made when she first learned she was dying. Jean Humphry wanted to die quietly at home beside her husband of more than twenty years. On a sunny March afternoon in 1975 she said goodbye, kissed him for the last time and drank a cup of coffee into which he had put a lethal drug. Telling his story on television, Mr Humphry said his wife chose the moment of death after she learned that the cancer had reached the top of her spine and was about to enter her brain.[7]

The availability of 'death on demand' could arrest the progress of medical science towards changing today's incurable or unbearable condition into the curable or bearable condition of tomorrow. It would also be difficult to ensure that there were sufficient safeguards to prevent abuse and the doctor's caring role could be seen as executioner rather than healer. Nurses, too, would not be above suspicion and the trust with which patients put their lives in our hands would be lost.

It is so difficult to get the balance quite right. The proportion of elderly people in the population is becoming a major cause of economic and social concern yet no longer content with the romantic setting where girl meets boy, falls in love, gets married and eventually conceives in the marital bed, we can now increase the population in a test tube in a laboratory. Scientists have already cloned mice and frogs so how long will it be before they are producing armies of identical humans by cloning? We could quite easily turn the whole process of reproduction into an exercise in chemistry.

Over the years, there has been considerable philosphical argument about the diagnosis of brain death; it was previously accepted that this occurred when the vital functions of respiration and circulation had ceased. How many night sisters have certified a patient dead when there was positive evidence that these functions had ceased? This, of course, was before the development of intensive care techniques which enable us to maintain these functions artificially. There is a well-established diagnostic criterion for brain death in the UK and this is applied when it becomes necessary to prove, beyond all doubt, that life has become extinct, e.g. in a patient who is a possible kidney donor.[8] However, the term 'dead' cannot always be taken literally; we hear of patients who 'came back from the dead' and a number of 'out of the body' experiences have been documented.

In the early morning of 20th December, 1943, a 20-year-old private soldier, George Ritchie, collapsed in front of an X-ray machine in an army hospital at Abilene, Texas and was rushed into an isolation room with a diagnosis of acute double pneumonia. Twenty-four hours later, the ward orderly found Ritchie apparently dead: breathing had stopped, there was no pulse or blood pressure. The duty medical officer checked, and told the orderly to prepare the body for the morgue after he had finished his rounds. He straightened Ritchie's arms along the blankets and pulled up the sheet to cover his face. About nine minutes later, the orderly returned and thought he saw a hand on the 'corpse' move. He fetched the doctor, who again pronounced Ritchie dead. Against all military and medical etiquette, the orderly suggested that the doctor should try giving a shot of adrenalin direct into the heart. Surprisingly, as he had twice pronounced Ritchie dead, the officer did so. The heart resumed its beat. On Christmas Eve, Ritchie recovered consciousness, and was back on his feet two weeks later. He went on to qualify as a doctor and psychiatrist.

Recounting his experience during the time he was 'dead' he remembered standing beside his bed looking down at his own body which was covered with a sheet. He had returned from a hectic journey across the United States. The light changed and brightened as he looked down at his body and he was surrounded by a living panorama of all the events of his life in completely clear detail. A figure came into the room ushering in a still more far-reaching journey. He returned from this to the pain of his illness when the adrenalin restarted his heart beating.[9]

Science has put into our hands quite remarkable powers. We can now cheat death mechanically and even in some cases bring patients back from the 'dead'. For the truly hopeless patient we can determine almost the exact time they will die by the gradually increased administration of drugs to prevent or relieve pain, in the sure knowledge that these drugs will also hasten death. The Law allows the termination of pregnancy, for a variety of reasons, procreation has become a matter of genetic engineering, and the remarkable progress made in transplant surgery seems to embody surgeons, in the eyes of the public, with an almost 'God-like' power.

We need to exercise great caution in using the powers we have been given; man has within himself the seeds of his own destruction and it is all too easy to lose sight of the values which really matter. We must not adopt an ostrich-like attitude when faced with the issues surrounding the terminally ill patient and his care. The nurse is the patient's advocate; he must be able to trust her, whether it be in the ward or in the theatre, in the sure knowledge that she will always do what is best for him. All too often, the dying patient is rejected as a failure, and we find it easier to busy ourselves with relatively unimportant tasks rather than face the challenge of giving comfort and support to the patient in what surely must be his greatest hour of need.

## Summary

The issues involved in caring for the terminally ill patient are many and complex and it is clear that there is no quick and easy answer. There is an urgent need for better preparation of nurses to enable them to cope with their own feelings towards death and dying and the particular needs of the patient. It is impossible to generalise on this important subject; however, it would be helpful if general ethical guidelines are formulated to protect individual human rights and maintain personal dignity.

Success should not always be measured in terms of cure; it can equally be achieved when we, as nurses, are privileged to use our professional expertise and human compassion in helping the dying patient, dealing appropriately with him, as we relate to patients in every aspect of life.

In our everyday professional work we deal in human life and whatever our personal inclinations may be, we will do well to remember that as the law stands, a positive act to cause or hasten death is murder, a criminal offence. The Law does not demand that a patient's life is artificially maintained when death is inevitable and is merely being postponed. When it comes to accepting treatment, all patients have the right of choice and this is no less true for the dying patient.

The ultimate decision for patient's treatment will be made by the doctor and it is the nurse's duty to administer this treatment. Nevertheless, she is, at all times, accountable for her professional actions and must not act against her own ethical or professional standards. Therefore, on some occasions, the solution may lie in doctors carrying out actions themselves.

**References and Note**

1. Marjorie Donahoe, 'Letter to a physician from a dying patient', *Ethicon/Point of View*, vol. 16, April 1979.
2. Evelyn C. Pearce, *A General Textbook of Nursing*, 9th ed., Faber & Faber 1945. Ch. 51, The nursing of the dying and care of the dead.
3. 'College sets up forum, for terminal care nurses', *Nursing Times*, 20 January 1982.
4. 'Doctor in mongol case is cleared', *Evening Standard*, 5 November 1981.
5. 'This baby must live!', *The Sun*, 8 August 1981.
6. 'Royal College welcomes acquittal of Down's baby case doctor', *Nursing Mirror*, 11 November 1981.
7. Jeff Bradley, 'She chose to die at home – with husband's help', *The Times-Picayune*, New Orleans, 14 March 1978.

8. Brain death: a Code of Practice has been prepared by a working party set up by the United Kingdom Health Departments under the Chairmanship of Lord Smith of Marlow, and revised by the available members of the Working Party, in the light of the further views expressed by the Conference of Medical Royal Colleges and Faculties of the United Kingdom on the diagnosis of brain death and other published evidence. See 'Cadaveric organs for transplantation,' 'A code of practice including the diagnosis of brain death'. Drawn up and revised by a working party on behalf of the Health Departments of Great Britain and Northern Ireland in February 1983.
9. John Davy, 'The evidence for life after death', *Observer Magazine*, 8 April 1979.

# 10 ORGAN TRANSPLANTATION

Pien Ch'iao, a Chinese gentleman and an honorable and cultured doctor of the third century B.C. is said to have carried a very special secret to his grave. Apparently he was on intimate terms with a pixie who helped him to see through the human body and diagnose disease. Once, because of the pixie's prompting, he gave two soldiers a knock-out brew of narcotic wine and when they were asleep, he opened them up and swapped over some of their internal organs including their hearts. When they awoke, some three days later, they were none the worse for the experience.[1]

William Hunter is reputed to have said that a surgeon is a savage armed with a knife, and when transplant surgery was in its infancy the pioneer surgeons were seen as little more, as they pursued their macabre exercises. Despite the enormous cost of the surgery, few patients survived for long and the whole idea of transplantation probably evoked more public controversy than any development in history. Apart from the obvious moral and ethical problems the public were more concerned about protecting their kidneys, and as this was the transplant operation which first attracted public attention, it gave the press a field-day. Horror stories hit the headlines of surgeons who allegedly were hunting around casualty departments looking for possible donors and the public's trust in doctors was temporarily damaged when it was suggested that some donors were not really dead.

The controversy surrounding diagnosis of death continued for years; it seemed that doctors could be trusted to recognise death in 'ordinary' patients but they had to prove that donors were 'dead dead' beyond all reasonable doubt. Until life-support machines entered routine hospital practice such a question was purely philosophical. Most student nurses could recognise the onset of death and it was quite acceptable for a senior sister to certify, verbally, that a patient was dead, particularly on night duty. The usual routine was that the eyes were closed, the limbs straightened, the body covered and left for a couple of hours before last offices were performed. Admittedly there was the occasional case of sudden or unexpected death but the pattern of disease was generally well established and there was little variation in treatment from one year to another.

Particularly in medical conditions, e.g. pneumonia and congestive heart failure, the patient's treatment relied heavily on good nursing care and for the acute conditions the 'crisis' was the turning-point. Either the patient made it then or all was lost. Tepid sponging, every three hours, plenty of fluids and a woollen blanket next to the patient to encourage sweating often succeeded in bringing the temperature down and from then on the patient was on the road to recovery.

Antibiotics have changed all this; now that it is possible to cure patients with tablets and injections, we have come to rely on them more and more. Present-day developments in the treatment of disease are the results of the work of far-seeing men of science, dedicated to improving the quality of life of patients, and biomedical research has afforded surgeons great knowledge and capability. Patients' expectations are now higher, and consequently many doctors have become conditioned to think only in terms of cure. Nevertheless, while it remains that many diseased organs cannot be cured, there are still many conditions for which transplantation offers the only hope.

It does not seem so many years ago that I watched helplessly as a patient of mine died by literally drowning in her own fluid. She had been given the most modern treatment available for patients in the terminal stage of renal failure but this was no more than palliative. She was born too early; a kidney transplant would have saved her and returned her to her husband and three little children; but this happened in 1950.

Christiaan Barnard achieved world fame almost overnight when he replaced the worn heart of Louis Washkansky, a Jew, with the healthy heart of a young white girl, but he also faced much criticism and misunderstanding, particularly in his own country, South Africa, divided as it is by colour and class. Despite all the efforts of the transplant team the patient died after 18 days but this did not deter Doctor Barnard from going ahead with his next heart transplant on Philip Blaiberg. The year was 1968.

In 1969, Donald Ross and Alan Yates gave Charles Hendrick a new heart at Guy's Hospital, London. Mr Hendrick lived for nine months after the operation but for much of this time he was dogged by infection – despite being given the heart of a nurse! However, at post-mortem, it was found that the transplanted heart was still healthy. Since that time, considerable progress has been made in technique and in coping with the problem of rejection and at Papworth Hospital, Cambridge, 51 heart transplants have been performed up to June 1983.[2] '"Every day is a bonus for us" said the wife of Paul Coffey, who in 1980 became the youngest man to have a heart transplant, and the 30th person in Britain to have this operation.'[3]

The argument will continue for years to come, whether it is more practical to consider the good of the majority or use available financial resources for the possible benefit of the few. Whatever the eventual outcome, transplantation surgery will continue. Throughout history there have been men of vision who, not content with the way things were, strived to improve the quality of life for mankind: Lister, Hunter, Fleming and Florey; these and many others introduced and perfected some revolutionary ideas and techniques, but initially few of their colleagues were prepared to accept them. The Church, too, was concerned about this so-called 'progress' and when it became known that Simpson was using chloroform for patients in childbirth, the Church of Scotland denounced its use in labour as unnatural and against the teachings of Scripture: 'Unto the woman he said, "I will greatly multiply thy sorrow and thy conception; in sorrow thou shalt bring forth children" ' (Genesis 3:16). Not to be outdone, Simpson retaliated by quoting the Bible: 'And the Lord God caused a deep sleep to fall upon Adam, and he slept; and He took one of his ribs and closed up the flesh thereof'. This then is an example of the opposition these great men faced but they were undaunted and today we have good reason to be grateful to them. Progress continued in this century when Magill and Rowbotham used the inhalation endotracheal method of anaesthesia when working with Sir Harold Gillies who performed now legendary surgery on war victims. In 1929 Tudor Edwards performed one of the first successful lower lobe lobectomies for cancer; Lane was knighted in 1913 for his many contributions to improved and safer surgery, and Cushing made it possible for surgeons to perform neurosurgery safely by the introduction of his little silver clips to stem the flow of bleeding.

Some people would argue that it is positively indecent even to consider a transplant programme when up and down the UK there are hundreds, probably thousands, of otherwise fit and healthy people who cannot properly contribute to the national economy because they have been waiting years to have a relatively simple operation, e.g. hernia repair, ligation of varicose veins. There are also others in the older age group who have to wait years for an operation which would remove their pain and give them a much improved quality of life. Total hip replacement offers hope to a great number of people but no doubt many of them will die before their turn for surgery comes.

Nearly 8,000 beds have been lost in the National Health Service since the Conservative government came to power in 1979, the House of Commons heard last week. In reply to a question put by Gwyneth Dunwoody, Junior Health Minister Geoffrey Finsberg released figures showing that since 1979, one hundred and nine hospitals have been completely closed and another 39 partially closed.[4]

It is in this climate that we must ask: are transplants a luxury we just cannot afford? They undoubtedly glamorise some surgeons but could also be considered an unnecessary drain on our already overstretched financial resources. Only in 1980 the Department of Health estimated that a heart transplant cost £17,500, so well might we wonder if our priorities are quite right.

In a country with unemployment running at four million people perhaps any available money should be spent on creating new industries which would give employment to the young, able-bodied, some who have never been able to find a job, rather than spending huge sums on the chronically sick with no guarantee of a cure. Maybe more of our money should be spent on preventive medicine, health education and the greater needs of the community at large, improving social conditions, better housing, more teachers to prevent the present disgraceful situation where some 16-year-olds now leave school hardly able to read or write. It is a sick society which places more importance on video machines and televisions than decent living conditions and education, but apathy can be engendered by unemployment and this in turn breeds indolence, aggression, law-breaking and a general lowering of standards. Maybe we should start now to prepare the present generation to avoid the mistakes of the past and help them to avoid perpetuating the present where all men are supposedly equal but some are still more equal than others.

Now, were it not for research, we would still think that the earth was flat and we would probably also be living in caves. The thirst for knowledge has spurred man on to find easier and better ways of doing things. It is said that when Queen Victoria had a 'wash tub' installed in Buckingham Palace, it was considered very daring, remembering that people had to take off all their clothes to get into it. When Alcock and Brown first flew the Atlantic, non-stop, in 1919, people gazed in amazement at 'the great big bird' in the sky. We take so much for granted when it comes to progress in our standard of living, so why should anyone resent the remarkable progress which has been made in the treatment of the sick?

Whether we like it or not, no one can deny that remarkable strides have been made in surgical procedures and the pace of medical advancement has been frighteningly fast in more recent years. With this progress have inevitably come problems: moral, ethical, legal, financial, political and economic. Because the progress came so fast, we have not always had time to deal with the problems. Some were not always apparent at the time, and some, like the diagnosis of brain death, were only seen as problems later.

The most popular transplant operations are for diseased kidneys and hearts, but while they have been well-publicised, many other transplantations have taken place both in the UK and abroad: heart and lung, testes, pancreas, liver, islets of Langerhans, bone marrow; and what about the 'baby banks' and 'baby farms'? If the word 'transplant' means transporting then this comparatively new method of increasing the population presents problems which affect the very basic laws of nature.

'We got our babies from a bank' said headmaster Carlton Duncan and his wife Sati and they were worth every penny of the £5,000 they borrowed from their bank manager. Mr Steptoe's revolutionary *in vitro* fertilisation provided this couple with beautiful twins who are now six months old. When, after three years of being childless, they realised that there was no chance of a normal pregnancy, they decided to consult Mr Steptoe, but before keeping the appointment with him, they had to find the money. The first attempt at fertilisation failed but the couple tried again the following year but again, failure. In order to find the cash for a third attempt, this couple 'went without holidays and cut down on entertaining and going out'.[5]

It has been reported that a Mrs Harriet Blankfield, an American businesswoman, was hoping to find suitable premises in London to start a 'baby farm' business where childless couples could have their own baby for the sum of £16,000.[6] The idea is that a surrogate mother would be artificially inseminated with the sperm of a husband whose wife was infertile. The problems associated with conventional organ transplantation pale into insignificance when one considers the multitude of horrendous situations which could result from this practice which could change the whole process of procreation and birth and destroy the structure of society as we know it today.

Shakespeare had a point when he said in *Henry VI*, 'let's kill all the lawyers'. It must be very frustrating for doctors who spend years hidden away in laboratories, burning the midnight oil in order to perfect a new technique, to then be told that it is illegal. No two disciplines develop at the same rate and it is inevitable that the Law will lag behind medicine, if only because there is never a guarantee that any new procedure will be successful, and it is only when it does succeed that the attending problems can be identified.

So who wins in the end? Will we create a brave new world where transplantation becomes simpler than repair? Will host mothers be more convenient for some people than pregnancy? Above all, who will decide?

## Problems Associated with Organ Transplantation

If the present knowledge is discriminately used it should eventually be possible to replace most body organs, except perhaps brain and gut, by transplantation. We will then have problems of identification; will John Smith remain the person he originally was or will his body become a container for a variety of other people's organs? Einstein said 'I am what I am because of my ductless glands'; what personality changes will the patient experience and how will the changes affect his relationships with his parents, wife, children and society?

There may have to be changes or additions to the marriage and divorce laws. Grounds for divorce might include concealing the number of transplants one or both partners have had, or the possible personality changes which may result from multiple transplants, causing the breakdown of a marriage.

It may be necessary, particularly for multiple organ recipients to carry identification cards stating the number and type of replaced organs. This would be particularly helpful in case of an accident. There will certainly be a need to reidentify allergies and psychological idiosyncracies of the new Id.

Some people may see the present interpretation of the Bible as outmoded, particularly Genesis 1: 26-28: 'And God said, Let us make man, wearing our own image and likeness; . . . So God made man in his own image, made him in the image of God. Man and woman both, he created them . . . increase and multiply and fill the earth, and make it yours'. Some Christian beliefs could become very confused; in a burial/cremation service, who will the deceased actually be and whose soul will leave the body at death? This last point will be of particular relevance for those who believe that the heart is the seat of the soul. If one believes in the resurrection of the body, who will rise from the dead on the Last Day, John Smith the whole person or a composite? It's worth thinking about.


**Legal Problems**

Despite the fact that transplantation surgery has been quite well established in the UK for some years the Law continues to be confused on many issues relating to it. This may not be such a bad thing and in many ways it could be quite reassuring to the public. We are still a democracy and the views and feelings of the people are taken into account, as far as possible, when new laws are passed. This is particularly true in regard to consent for donor organs and unlike some other countries, permission of surviving relatives is sought before any organ is removed from a deceased for the purpose of transplantation, that is unless there is evidence that the deceased had indicated in life that he wished his body or particular organs to be so used after his death, e.g. a kidney donor card or other such evidence.

It has been known for people to state in their will that they wish their bodies to be used for medical purposes after their death. Obviously this is of no value regarding certain organs, such as kidneys or heart, for transplantation. The usual practice is that a will is not read until some time after a death and unless there is a relative available who has knowledge of the will (beneficiaries are not allowed to witness a will) then valuable time is lost.[7] Even when there is immediate evidence that a dying patient wishes his body to be so used after his death, it is still considered good practice in the UK to discuss this tactfully with the nearest relative. If the relative objects, despite the wishes of the deceased, 'staff will need to judge according to the circumstances of the case whether it is wise to proceed with organ removal'.[8] The Human Tissue Act 1961 and the Human Tissue Act (Northern Ireland) 1962 gives to 'the person lawfully in possession of the body' the right to object to the body, or parts of the body (of the deceased) being used for medical purposes, e.g. transplantation.

Considerable and prolonged discussion has taken place regarding what came to be known as 'the dilemma of brain death'. There is now a strict agreed criteria for this diagnosis (see p. 93) and I do not see any necessity to dwell on it further.

## Live Related Donor

There does not appear to be any statute directly relating to the rights of a donor. Theoretically, we are each the owners of our own body to do with it what we will. In practice, the donor signs a consent for the operation to remove a healthy kidney, but not before the implications of this particular procedure are clearly explained. In legal terms, this operation could be termed 'maiming'. However:

> Lord Justice Davies gave his opinion, speaking extra-judicially, that he would be surprised if a surgeon were successfully sued for trespass to the person or convicted of causing bodily harm to one of full age and intelligence who freely consented to act as donor – always provided that the operation did not present unreasonable risk to the donor's life or health.[9]

The general rule for donors in the UK is that they must have attained 18 years and be of sound mind and good general health before being considered as a possible donor. With patients who come from abroad requiring a transplant, the surgeon uses his professional judgement regarding the age of the donor. If, in his opinion, the only way in which he can offer the patient the chance to live, is by accepting a kidney from a consenting minor, then the operation will be performed. Minor in this case would mean a young person between 14 and 18 years old. This, theoretically, contravenes section 8 of the Family Law Reform Act 1969, but this has yet to be tested in a court of Law.

The story is told by a well-known English transplant surgeon of a male patient of his who required a kidney transplant. The man's daughter rushed from America ready to save her father's life by offering her kidney. After submitting to various tests the unexpected evidence emerged that she was not, in fact, her father's daughter. Not wishing to create a further family crisis, the wise surgeon kept this information to himself.

**Heart Transplantation: the Problems**

The legal ruling for removal of a cadaver heart is exactly the same as for removal of a cadaver kidney and the Human Tissue Act applies. One of the criteria for selection for transplantation is that the recipient must come from a stable background. The most pressing practical problems are shortage of money, facilities, doctors and nurses.

**Corneas**

It has long been the practice in the UK for people to arrange during their lifetime that their eyes be removed after death so that a blind person may see. There is little public emotion about this well-established arrangement and 'eye banks' are maintained in at least 12 regions. Eyes are always needed for corneal grafting and further details can be obtained from the Royal National Institute for the Blind. It is not essential that eyes are 'willed' but the conditions, as outlined in the Human Tissue Act 1961, apply with regard to permission of relatives. There is rarely any problem with regard to diagnosis of brain death in donors. Eyes can be removed and subsequently used up to 12 hours after death; if the body has been kept in a refrigerated mortuary, the period can be extended to 24 hours. The Code of Practice states that it is not necessary to have operating theatre conditions for removal; however, the eyes must be removed by an appropriately trained person but not necessarily a fully trained surgeon.

## Bone Marrow Transplant

As yet there is no particular ruling regarding the age of consent for donors in this relatively new form of transplantation, as illustrated by the following news item: 'The first person to donate bone marrow at the new Regional Bone Marrow Transplant Service in Leeds was five-year-old Kelly Hutchinson. Her sister Karen, aged nine, was the grateful recipient.'[10]

## Artificial Reproduction: the Problems

There are a number of types of artificial reproduction available: artificial insemination by the husband; artificial insemination by donor; sperm bank artificial insemination by donor or husband; egg grafts (for women who have no ovaries); *in vitro* fertilisation; and surrogate mothers or 'womb-leasing'

### Artifical Insemination by the Husband

From the legal viewpoint, artificial insemination by husband poses few problems. Both partners have the procedure explained to them and they are then asked to sign consent forms if they agree to proceed with the treatment. Any problems which occur are more likely to be psychological, particularly if a successful pregnancy does not result. Serious psychosexual problems may well be the cause of inability to conceive and couples are given a psychological screening before AIH is considered.

### Artificial Insemination by Donor

This method has been successfully used for some years to improve the quality of livestock, e.g. seminal fluid removed from a sire may be successfully diluted at least 8 times and used to produce many more horses than by natural mating. In humans

AID poses many potential legal problems. It could be considered adultery as the wife is receiving the seed of a third party and her husband might possibly have grounds for divorce because of this. Legally, any child born by AID will be illegitimate and therefore would not be the rightful son and heir to any property settled by succession. The donor in AID must sign a waiver of rights in any child which is produced from his semen and doctors insist on strict donor anonymity. The couple have the right legally to adopt the child but of course this will have to be stated on the revised birth certificate. This may well cause psychological problems for the child once he finds out that his father is not in fact his father. Couples who submit to AID need to have a very stable relationship and it may be that at a later time the husband may have feelings of inadequacy or even jealousy because of his possible inability to produce children of his own. These feelings may well affect his relationship with the child.

AID may result in many anonymous fathers in society and it is possible that unknown incestuous relationships may exist because of this.

## Sperm Bank AID

This could prove to be the most frightening form of artificial reproduction and it has endless possibilities. When sperm is stocked by AID, the donor will contribute at his convenience. Matching will be more streamlined and unusual types of sperm can be stored thereby allowing a choice of race, height, blood group and perhaps certain desirable characteristics. An entire new race of people could be produced by this method.

Husbands can also store sperm in this bank for use at a later date and I know of at least one case in the USA where a husband stored sperm in such a bank when he knew he was dying. After his death, the sperm was transplanted into his widow who ultimately produced a healthy baby boy. The risk of possible incestuous relationships being formed between offsprings of AID is a definite problem and this in turn could increase the incidence of genetically inherited disease.

## Egg Grafts

For women who are without ovaries, or who have non-functioning ovaries, a ripe egg can be supplied by a donor woman. This egg is implanted in the Fallopian tubes and subsequently fertilised by the man. It might be that the donor could be said to have some legal right to any baby born by this method, irrespective of whether or not she had signed an agreement to the contrary.

## In Vitro *Fertilisation*

It was in July 1978 that the first test tube baby was born in the UK, the first time that a baby was conceived in a piece of glass. Since that time a number of babies have been produced by this method, which has raised a number of legal and ethical problems. The legal problem is quite straightforward: whether or not the practice should be allowed to continue. The ethical problems are more complicated.

## *Surrogate Mothers or 'Womb-leasing'*

Isolated cases of womb-leasing have been reported for some years but more recently it has been recognised as a lucrative business. It would seem unreasonable to make laws to cover every possible eventuality and therefore at the moment no law exists either to permit or disallow this practice. Recently, evidence from a Law Society committee was given to the Warnock Inquiry, which was set up by the Department of Health to investigate the ethics of human fertilisation, including test tube babies. It is likely that the 1984 findings of their Inquiry will frame future laws relating to artificial reproduction.

Again, with this form of reproduction there will inevitably be problems, some of which will be difficult to solve. Will the father and surrogate mother be the 'natural' parents? What legal rights will the surrogate mother have in relation to the child she has carried for 9 months? If there is evidence of malformation of the baby during pregnancy, who will have the right to decide on abortion? How difficult will it be to monitor the surrogate mother to ensure that she does not smoke, drink alcohol or take drugs and if she does indulge, could she be charged with wilful negligence?

There could also be the problem that the surrogate mother may change her mind and decide to keep the baby; if this happens, and a couple have already paid for the procedure, what is their legal right to sue? Will they sue the person to whom the money was paid or can they take legal action against the surrogate mother for the return of the now developed foetus, the baby, for which the husband was at least partly responsible? There can be no doubt that morally any baby born must belong to the mother and father, i.e. the husband of the infertile woman and the surrogate mother, no matter how this child was conceived. This knowledge must affect the child both socially and psychologically – that is unless this practice became accepted as a normal method of reproduction.

> And still Abram's wife Sarai bore him no children. But she had an Egyptian maid-servant, called Agar; and now she said to her husband, The Lord, as thou seest, denies me motherhood; betake thyself to this maid of mine, in the hope that I may at least have children through her means. So Abram consented to the wish of his wife. . . . Abram then had knowledge of her, and she, finding herself with child, began to look on her mistress with scorn . . . and she bore a son to Abram, and called him Ismael; Abram was eighty-six years old at the time of Ismael's birth. (Genesis 16: 1-5, 14-16.

## Moral Problems of Transplantation

The views of a number of religious beliefs concerning transplantation have already been stated in Chapter 4. The Christian churches recognise the value to society of progress in medicine but there is a marked division in doctrine between the Church of England and the Roman Catholic Church relating to artificial reproduction. Within the Church of England itself there is a diversity of approach and a range of opinion to this controversial development. Formal discussion takes place on any new development which may have a moral/ethical implication, but at the moment no définite views have been formulated or comprehensive statement issued regarding artificial reproduction.

The doctrine of the Roman Catholic Church continues to be unchanged and is as restated by Pope Pius XII in 1969. In rejecting artificial insemination as a method of procreation he said that 'it would convert the domestic hearth and sanctuary of the family into nothing more than a biological laboratory'. Artificial insemination is banned by Lutheran churches and also by Orthodox Jews.

**Summary**

Once upon a time there were quacks, apothecaries and men of physic. Then in 1745, the surgeons set themselves up as a separate group from the barbers but their methods were still viewed with suspicion and most forms of disease continued to be treated by the physicians. Lack of anatomical knowledge meant that many regions of the body were inaccessible to the surgeon's knife. Gradually all this changed and today there are no anatomical barriers; anything is possible.

Transplantation, in all its forms, probably poses more problems than any other development in surgery; it can be frightening to the public yet challenging to the surgeon. But whatever the problems, there are many people today who owe their lives to the surgeon's skill and dedication. Nursing today is no longer a matter of just soothing the fevered brow; it is about professionalism, accountability, management, research and education. Somewhere in the middle of all this there are sick people who today have more alternative treatments available for their illness than ever before. They need nurses who must keep in mind the impact that today's decisions will have on tomorrow's practice; nurses with sufficient political and professional 'muscle' to ensure that their voice is heard and their views respected.

Legislation has intruded into all our lives and today's nurse must have a sound knowledge to enable her to question the ethical and legal implications of her work. The lives we touch should be richer for our care and our overriding attitude a reverence for human life. Nevertheless, it must be accepted that transplantation is no longer in its embryonic stage and present results are encouraging. The way forward is now clear for further developments in this field and the fact that there will be growing legal and ethical problems will not halt progress.

**Acknowledgements**

My thanks are due to the following for help in preparing this chapter: Mr Alan Yates, Consultant Cardio-Thoracic Surgeon, Guy's Hospital, London; Mr C. Rudge, Consultant Renal Surgeon, Guy's Hospital; Father J. Lennon, Parish Priest, St Stephen's Catholic Church, Welling, Kent; Canon G. Telford, Parish Priest, Holy Trinity Catholic Church, Dockhead, London SE1; Rev. E. Martin, Church of England Chaplain

Guy's Hospital; Father E. Holloway, Parish Priest, Roman Catholic Church, Claygate, Surrey; Mr J. Gladwin, Secretary to the Board of the Church of England Synod.

# References

1. Robert G. Richardson, *The Surgeon's Tale*, George Allen & Unwin, 1958.
2. 'Survivor of new heart miracle', *Surrey Comet*, 27 May 1983.
3. 'Every day is a bonus for us', *Nursing Times*, 11 May 1983.
4. 'NHS has lost nearly 8000 beds', *Nursing Times*, 18 May 1983.
5. 'We got our babies from a bank', *The Sun*, 4 February 1983.
6. 'Stop the baby farms', *The Universe*, 22 April 1983.
7. Wills Act 1837; see also Wills Act 1968.
8. 'A Code of practice. The removal of cadaveric organs for transplantation', drawn up by a working party on behalf of the Health Departments of Great Britain and Northern Ireland, October 1979, p. 8, IV: Approach to relatives.
9. W.A.J. Farndale, *Law on Human Transplants and Bequests of Bodies*, vol. 2, Ravenswood Publications, Beckenham, 1970. Case study no. 7, p. 39, (a) living donors.
10. 'First donor for unit', *Nursing Mirror*, 3 November 1982.

# Further Reading

Christiaan Bernard and Bill Curtis Pepper, *One Life*, Harrap, 1969.

R.Y. Calne, *Clinical Organ Transplantation*, Blackwell Scientific Publications, 1971.

Michael Debakey, M.D., and Antonio Gotto, M.D., *The Living Heart*, Charter Books, 1977.

James M. Dunlop, 'Genetic engineering', *Nursing Times*, 5 February 1976.

Donald Logmore, *Spare-part Surgery*, Aldus Books, 1968.

'Artificial reproduction', *Nursing Times*, 4 April 1974.

Social Welfare Commission of the Catholic Bishop's Conference (England and Wales), 'Human fertilisation – choices for the future', evidence to the government enquiry into human fertilisation and embryology, March 1983.

Robert M. Veatch, *Case Studies in Medical Ethics*, 6th printing, Harvard University Press, 1980.

# 11 THE CORONER'S COURT

The office of coroner is one of the oldest in England, dating back to the twelfth century. At that time, the duties of the coroner, or 'crowner' as he was called, were much wider than they are today. He had the power to seize treasure-trove in the king's name and take possession of wrecks, stranded whales and royal sturgeons. He was also responsible for collecting and guarding certain revenues of the king, seeking out criminals, extorting confessions from them and confiscating their goods for the crown. He tried 'appeals' or accusations of felony and investigated deaths from violence. Coroners ranked second only to the sheriff in importance in a county and their office was created from a widespread desire to curtail the sheriff's powers, which were being greatly abused. One rather unusual way of holding office was by virtue of possessing a horn, and it was not unknown for a family to hold the office by inheritance as owners of an 'instrument of summons'. More generally, the office was confined to only 'most wise discreet and lawful knights' and was unpaid until 1488 when a fee of 13s 4d was allowed for each murder inquest.

In 1276, the statute *De Officia Coronatoris* set out the coroner's duties in detail but this statute was repealed by the consolidating Coroner's Act 1887, which more fully defined the coroner's duty of inquiry into unexplained death. An amendment to the Act in 1926 obviated the necessity of a coroner having to empanel a jury for every inquest and with the exception of certain specific cases where he had no option, he was allowed to decide whether or not to sit with a jury.

## Eligibility for Office

Coroners in the main have to be either doctor, solicitor or barrister of at least five years' standing and many have dual qualifications. In Metropolitan London the dual qualification of doctor and barrister is required; provincial coroners must be either a doctor or a solicitor. Appointments are made by the county council in which the jurisdiction lies but the appointing authority has no control over the coroner and he is answerable for his professional behaviour in this office only to the Lord Chancellor.

## Purpose and Function of the Coroner's Court

One of the most important functions of the court is to investigate any sudden or unexplained death. While there is no legally enforceable duty on a doctor to report any death to the coroner he does have a legal duty to issue a certificate stating the cause of death and this certificate is then given to the Registrar of Births and Deaths. The form of death certificate is prescribed by the Registration Regulations and must state: the immediate cause of death and morbid conditions, if any, giving rise to the immediate cause, stated in order proceeding backwards from the immediate cause; any other morbid conditions contributing but not related to the immediate cause.[1]

A doctor is only required to issue a death certificate if he has been in attendance on a patient during his last illness. If, despite having attended the deceased the doctor is unable to state the cause of death, he should then report the fact to the coroner. A false statement on a death certificate is perjury, an offence punishable by fine and imprisonment under the Perjury Act 1911. It is the duty of the Registrar to report to the coroner any death registered with him, the details of which give rise to suspicion.

## Instructions to Doctors

The Medical Protection Society has issued the following instructions regarding the types of deaths which should be reported to the coroner:

1. All deaths which are sudden or unexpected and where the doctor cannot certify the real as opposed to the terminal cause of death or where the doctor has not attended in the last illness of within fourteen days of death.
2. Abortions – other than natural.
3. Accidents and injuries of any date if in any way contributing to the cause of death.

4. Anaesthetics and operations, i.e. death whilst under the influence of anaesthetics, and deaths following operations for injuries, or where the operation, however necessary or skilfully performed, may have precipitated or expedited death.

5. Crime or suspected crime.

6. Drugs – therapeutic or addiction.

7. Ill-treatment – starvation or neglect.

8. Industrial disease arising out of the deceased's employment, e.g. pneumoconiosis, Weils' disease, all disease covered by the Health and Safety at Work Act 1974.

9. Infant deaths – if in any way obscure.

10. Pensioners receiving disability pensions where death may be connected with a pensionable disability.

11. Persons in legal custody – in prison, borstal institutions or detention centres.

12. Poisoning from any source.

13. Septicaemia, if originating from an injury.

14. Stillbirths, where there may be the possibility of the child having been born alive or where there is suspicion.[2]

Additional to this list are patients who die within 24 hours of receiving an anaesthetic, the death of known alcoholics (alcohol is classed as a poison in law), and also persons who die as the result of a fracture (pulmonary embolus may well kill the patient, but this is secondary to the fracture which would be the primary cause of death, i.e. no fracture, then no embolus).

Medicine and nursing are two distinct disciplines, but it is doctors and nurses who are primarily responsible for the care of patients in hospitals. If we are to combine our expertise for the patient's benefit then information such as given above should be known by all nurses and should be included in every basic training programme. Let us now examine some of these circumstances from the theatre nurse's viewpoint.

**Sudden Death**

A fit and healthy patient can die in the time it takes to transport him from the ward to the anaesthetic room and although in many cases the doctor will probably be able to certify the real cause of death, there may be occasions when this is not so.

## Accidents and Injuries

Eternal vigilance is the price of safety and if this principle is not applied there are many instances where accidents and injuries can contribute to a patient's death. Some of these include: retained foreign bodies; incorrect positioning on a trolley or the operating table; patients left unattended, in the anaesthetic room or recovery room; diathermy burns; the use of explosive anaesthetic agents with diathermy; burns caused by instruments which have been sterilised and not allowed to cool; rough handling of patients whose disability is not known to theatre staff, e.g. arthrodesed joint, arthritis, bone metastases.

Accidents can also be caused by carelessness when little or no attention is paid to detail, e.g. incorrect temperature of the theatre, dispensing with counts during an operation, omitting to check the patient's identity, and ignorance, when a nurse performs any task for which she has not had prior instruction.

## Anaesthetics and Operations

The National Association of Theatre Nurses, and indeed many anaesthetists, advocate that the patient in the anaesthetic room should be attended by a nurse; be that as it may, whoever is responsible for the patient's care should ensure that there is no margin of error in the preparation of drugs and anaesthetic gases. *All* drugs *must* be checked and administered by the anaesthetist and this admonition cannot be repeated too often. Far too many cases of negligence in this area have been documented: 'Hospital's blunder op killed a wife'. This news item told of the death of a 41-year-old woman during a routine operation. It was 14 months after the operation before her husband was told what really happened; two breathing machines failed to work because a girl trainee had assembled them wrongly, the anaesthetist had trouble with needles and tripped over wires, and the patient lay on the operating table for two minutes without oxygen. The Health Authority in this case admitted liability and the husband was paid a total of £50,000.

All duties during the operation must be carried out conscientiously, with the patient's well being in mind. If, however, the patient dies the nursing staff will at least know that nothing in their conduct contributed to his death.

## Drugs

A large number of drugs are used in the operating theatre and the task of recognition is often complicated by the existence of two or more sometimes dissimilar names for each preparation: an approved name, one or more proprietary names and also a full chemical name. To add to this confusion the use of abbreviations further increases the risk of error, e.g. 'sux' for Suxamethonium, 'thio' for thiopentone.

Mistakes in the preparation and administration of drugs can undoubtedly lead to a patient's untimely death. These mistakes can happen when verbal instructions are given in an emergency or when the staff involved do not have a common first language. It is equally true that some written instructions are indecipherable and tragic accidents can occur when a decimal point is in the wrong place or has simply been forgotten; all the more reason for double-checking. All ampoules used in theatre look much the same and no matter how urgent the need, the label must be checked every time an ampoule is removed from a box. If the findings at an inquest prove that a patient's death was caused or precipitated by the administration of an inaccurate amount of a drug or indeed the wrong drug, then the staff who prepared and administered the drug will be called to give evidence. The Health Authority is responsible for the professional actions of its employees but this of course does not absolve the person in charge, e.g. the theatre sister, and also the member of staff responsible for the incident.

## Ill-treatment

It must surely be the fervent hope of every nurse that ill-treatment will never be given as the cause of death of any hospital patient. However, in certain cases, lack or absence of treatment can constitute ill-treatment. Recently, much public attention has been given to allegations concerning a small number of geriatric and psychiatric patients. These allegations implied that there was an element of ill-treatment in the patients' care. It is all too easy to be critical, forgetting the acute shortage of nurses in these areas, the emotional and physical strain of the work and, in some cases, the often violent and aggressive behaviour of some of the unfortunate patients. In all but a few of the cases, no proof of ill-treatment was found.

## Industrial Disease

It is not uncommon for patients suffering from communicable diseases to require surgery. The Health and Safety at Work Act 1974 states (ch. 37) that this is

> an Act to make provision for securing the health, safety and welfare of persons at work, for protecting others against risk to health or safety in connection with the activities of persons at work, for controlling the keeping and use and preventing the unlawful acquisition, possession and use of dangerous substances, and for controlling certain emissions into the atmosphere, to make further provision with respect to the employer and medical advisory service, to amend the law relating to building regulations and the building (Scotland) Act 1959 and for connected purposes.

Subsection 2 (3) requires the employer to issue 'a written statement of his general policy with respect to health and safety at work of his employees and the organisation and arrangements for the time being in force for carrying out that policy, and to bring the statement and any revision of it to the notice of all his employees'.

In caring for patients with communicable diseases the theatre nurse herself is at risk and this section of the Act makes it clear that the employer has a duty to ensure that there are adequate safety precautions for her protection. Surgery is her 'industry' and inherent in it there is always the risk of infection. Viral hepatitis is a prescribed occupational disease in Britain and the Royal College of Nursing has warned that 'the evidence of nurses contracting viral hepatitis due to their working environment is on the increase. . .'[3] 'In laboratory reports on acute viral hepatitis for 1975-9, 287 staff with acute hepatitis B infection were reported. Three deaths were reported of which two were women nurses and one was a male dental surgeon.'[4]

## Infant Deaths and Stillbirths

It is the practice in many hospitals to transport an infant to and from theatre in his cot and he is normally returned to his cot immediately after surgery. Over the years, enormous publicity has been given to some unexplained 'cot deaths' and a number of theories have been advanced in an attempt to understand why this happens. It is of paramount importance that the infant being cared for in the recovery ward is never left alone, even when he is considered to have regained consciousness.

The term 'stillbirth' applies to any foetus which has issued forth from the mother after the 28th week of pregnancy and has not had a separate existence, i.e. has not taken oxygen into the lungs. The theatre nurse will do well to be clear in her own mind about the condition of any foetus delivered by Caesarean section at which she assists and her actions must be above suspicion.

## Inquests

When a doctor decides that a patient's death must be reported to the coroner, it may be on the results of a post-mortem examination that the coroner will decide that an inquest is not necessary. If this is so, the Coroner's Officer will inform the Registrar of the cause of death and the death can then be registered. If, on the other hand, the coroner has reasonable cause to suspect that death was caused or precipitated by violent or unnatural causes, he will then order an inquest. This may be held without a jury but if there is evidence that death has been caused by an accident or a disease of which notice has to be given to the government, e.g. industrial accident, or if the deceased died in prison, then there has to be a jury. In other cases, the coroner may summon a jury if he thinks it would be of assistance.

Jurors are selected from the electoral roll and a jury may be comprised of from 7 to 11 people. The coroner may wish to view the body but the jury need not do so unless the coroner so directs or a majority of the jury so decide. It is the coroner who decides which witnesses should be summoned to give evidence and his general power allows him to compel the attendance of such witnesses as he deems necessary. Non-attendance of summoned witnesses will only be accepted if just cause can be shown for not obeying the order. If it is alleged that the actions of a nurse may have contributed to a patient's death then she may be called to give evidence.

It is a wise precaution for any nurse in this situation to seek advice and guidance from her senior manager and her professional organisation. If she tells the truth she has nothing to fear; however, the process of law, as administered in the courts, can be confusing to the uninformed, and sometimes quite frightening. When questions posed require a direct yes/no answer, she must resist the temptation to explain the whole series of events which led to the particular incident, e.g. shortage of staff, overwork, inexperienced nurses performing tasks for which they have not had instruction. However much the coroner may wish to sympathise with the nurse's problems, he is well aware of the absolute necessity for high standards of patient care and can hardly be expected to condone a situation where standards are allowed to fall below an acceptable level. An inquest is an enquiry, not a trial, and its purpose is to establish, beyond all reasonable doubt, the cause of death.

In the few cases where the enquiry shows that death could be due to murder, manslaughter or infanticide, and a person has been charged accordingly, the inquest is adjourned for 18 months, thus allowing time for the Crown Court trial to take place. The Crown Court trial replaces the inquest (even if the prisoner is acquitted) and the result of the trial is sent to the coroner. In the event of no persons being charged with the crime after 18 months, the inquest is reopened and the usual verdict returned is that the crime was committed by person or persons unknown. The papers for the prosecution are sent to the Director of Public Prosecution via Scotland Yard's Solicitor's Office prior to the inquest.[5]

Particularly in cases of death due to negligence, the coroner has a preventive role in bringing to the notice of the appropriate authorities, employers and indeed the public, the danger of continuing the practice which led to the death, thus preventing a recurrence. Apart from those involving national security, all inquests are held in public and the press are allowed to be present.

When a coroner directs that a post-mortem should be performed, whether or not he deems an inquest necessary, it is not necessary for him to obtain the permission of relatives. If, for any reason, relatives have strong objections, they have the right to swear out a prayer of Habeas Corpus at the Queen's Bench division of the High Court, but as this takes six weeks and does not automatically guarantee success, such action is rarely taken: If, however, this procedure proves successful, the post-mortem is held back pending the court's decision.

### Post-mortem

In our enlightened age, the post-mortem has become an essential part of research and medical advancement. Many people direct during life that they wish their body to be used for anatomical dissection after death, and section 1(1) of the Human Tissue Act 1961 provides the following:

> If any person in writing at any time or orally in the presence of two or more witnesses during his last illness, has expressed a request that his body or any specified part of his body be used after his death for therapeutic purposes or for purposes of medical education or research, the person lawfully in possession of his body after death may, unless he has reason to believe that the request was subsequently withdrawn, authorise the removal from the body of any part or of, as the case may be, the specified part, for use in accordance with the request.

Section 1(2) of the Act makes it clear that even if the deceased has not made arrangements as described in section 1(1), the person in charge of the body may give consent, as outlined in section 1(1), unless he has knowledge that the deceased had expressed an objection to his body being so dealt with after death.

It is quite ethical for a doctor to request permission from relatives to carry out a post-mortem on any patient who has died in hospital. Much useful information can be gained from this and it is an excellent learning exercise for medical students. The Human Tissue Act 1961 stipulates that 'the removal of any part of a body . . . is not to be effected except by a fully registered medical practitioner, who must have satisfied himself by personal examination of the body that life is extinct', and a condition of the Anatomy Act 1832 is 'that the removal for anatomical

117

examination does not take place until 48 hours after death. . . .'
In the event of relatives refusing permission for a post-mortem it
would be most improper to then refer the case to the coroner. As
previously stated, relatives' permission is not required for a
coroner's post-mortem and this applies even if the examination is
contrary to the religious beliefs of the deceased.

The Anatomy Act 1832 (minor amendment 1871) put paid to
the practice of 'body-snatching', a lucrative business which
persisted up to the last century. 'The master of a workhouse
showed the bodies of the deceased to their relatives and then
arranged for each, the appearance of a funeral. When the
relatives had departed the bodies were transferred to a well-
known London Medical School for anatomical dissection'.[6]
Interestingly enough, this workhouse master was not found guilty
of a crime because under section 7 of the Act, 'he had lawful
possession of the bodies' and none of the relatives had stated that
they required burial without dissection. It must be said in his
favour that having collected his fee and when the dissection was
complete, he did at least have the remains buried.

When the coroner is satisfied that the cause of death has been
established and no other reason exists why disposal of the body
should not take place, the Coroner's Officer informs the Registrar
that the death can be registered and directs the relatives that
burial or cremation can take place. It is illegal to disinter any
human remains unless under licence from the Secretary of State:
however, a rather unusual case of exhumation occurred as late as
1960. In December of that year a young man was prosecuted for
removing the remains of his mother from her grave. Apparently
he was with her during her last illness and did everything he
possibly could to bring about her recovery. He even applied
electric treatment as a last resort when she was *in extremis*, but
all to no avail. Thinking about this later, he decided that it might
be worthwhile having another go, so one late evening he dug up
her coffin and removed her body to a safe place. For a whole
week he tried unsuccessfully to feed her with a mixture of
plasma, sugar, lime juice and milk. Realising that this would not
produce the desired effect, he decided to recommence the
electric treatment. He carefully connected one of her legs to the
household electrical system but unfortunately there was a short-
circuit. This man was later found to be suffering from mental
disorder.[7]

118

## Danger of Infection and Last Offices

All nurses need reminding that when they perform Last Offices there are still a number of precautions which must be taken. Infection does not die with the patient and consideration must be given to the many people who may have to handle the body when it leaves the ward or unit. All information relating to any infectious disease from which the patient may have been suffering should be written on a card attached to the shroud. When packing orifices it is important that the rectum is not packed too tightly; cotton wool has been left in the descending colon before now, and this has only been found when the specimen has been sent for culture.

The practice of wrapping the body in a sheet which is secured with safety pins, still persists in many hospitals. The safety pins only hamper the work of the post-mortem room or mortuary technician; adhesive tape is much more effective and easier and quicker to remove. No doubt springing from the Christian tradition, it has long been the custom to cross the arms on the chest or join the hands together. While there are some religions which insist on this, it is much more helpful if the arms are placed straight down by the sides.

The Howie Report (1978, periodically updated) has recommended certain safeguards for the protection of staff, notably in medical laboratories and post-mortem rooms, but the information contained therein will be of value to all nurses. There are already strict regulations governing the design and facilities of mortuaries and this Report seeks to ensure that staff take every precaution to avoid infection including:

(a) The wearing of gowns and gloves, and in some cases visors, when dealing with infected material.

(b) The use of appropriate disinfectants as cleaning agents when dealing with particular infected tissues e.g. tuberculosis, hepatitis B.

(c) A ventilation change of 10 volumes of air per hour in the post-mortem room.

(d) Only staff who are Mantoux-positive to be allowed in the mortuary when a case of tuberculosis is being autopsied.

(e) A limited examination, confined to the kidneys or other relevant organs in cases of hepatitis B. All renal dialysis cases will be expected to have been screened for Australia antigen and this information must be confirmed by the renal unit in every case.

(f) Under no circumstances will an autopsy be performed on even suspected cases of Category A pathogens, e.g. Lassa fever, Marburg or Green Monkey disease, smallpox, rabies.

The Howie Report states that it is the responsibility of the consultant in charge of the case to notify the appropriate staff of any infection or other hazard, of cases coming to autopsy. In the case of transmissible infection, the corpse should be enclosed in a plastic bag before being removed from the ward and relatives should be discouraged from viewing the corpse.

It is understandable that when a nurse is carrying out Last Offices she will wish to do everything possible to ensure that the remains are prepared as tastefully as possible; however, she must at all times remember the 'golden rule': *never* remove anything from the body, e.g. drain, catheter, intravenous infusion, tracheostomy tube, unless specifically instructed to do so. These are visual evidence of particular treatments and may prove to be vital evidence if an inquest becomes necessary. If the patient has had a radium implant or pacemaker, this information should be included on the card attached to the shroud.

All the property found with the deceased should be checked with another member of staff and entered in the appropriate book. This procedure acts as a safeguard if the nurse checks any valuables, e.g. jewellery, on the body before and after the remains have been viewed by relatives. It has been known for the relatives to remove property and enquire as to its whereabouts at a later date. If for any reason a swab is deliberately left in a patient during surgery this should be recorded in the notes. Should a post-mortem become necessary much time and worry will be saved when it can be proved that the swab was deliberately left in.

The nurse working in an accident and emergency department should be acquainted with the procedure regarding reception and care of patients who may become the subject of court proceedings, e.g. cases of stabbing, shooting or drug overdose. Any of these patients may die on admission and if the police are not already present it is the duty of the nurse in charge to contact them. Once death has been certified, it is imperative that no one touches the body until the police arrive. Ideally, the body should be kept in a locked room and all clothes and belongings of the deceased retained until the police arrive. The police will also require any blood which has been taken e.g. for cross-matching. Blood contaminated with, for example, adrenalin, is of no use for alcohol trace.

## The Procedure in Scotland

There are many similarities between the Scottish and English legal systems but by the Treaty of Union 1707 the Scots have been allowed to keep their own legal system. The office of Procurator Fiscal carries many responsibilities and considerable authority. Among other duties he is responsible for inquiring into causes of suspicious deaths. However, unlike the system in England, the Procurator conducts his enquiry in private. Deaths which must be reported to the Procurator include: deaths during an operation performed under, or during, administration of either a local or general anaesthetic; deaths which are considered clinically to be due to an anaesthetic; and deaths within 12 hours of an operation performed under a general anaesthetic.

He will also require the following information from an independent doctor who is experienced in anaesthetics or pathology: if the patient was examined pre-operatively; whether all normal precautions were taken in the administration of the anaesthetic; if there were any factors which could have been discovered by examination that indicated a special risk in the administration of the anaesthetic; and whether the patient was kept under constant medical and/or nursing care during the post-operative period.

A Scottish death certificate does not require the certifying doctor to have been in attendance on the patient before death and it is not required for him to have seen the body after death. The Cremation Act 1902 applies in both England and Scotland and a death certificate must be issued and the death registered before cremation can take place.[8]

Oyez! Oyez! Oyez! All manner of persons who have anything to do at this court before the Queen's Coroner for this county, touching the death of . . . draw near and give your attention.

This is the proclamation, dating back to the twelfth century, for the opening of an inquest when a jury is present.

## Summary

This brief overview of the work of the coroner and his court can only serve to acquaint the reader with information which requires more detailed elaboration and therefore further reading is advised. The coroner is vested with considerable authority and his court is the first instance for inquiring into and determining the cause of death in certain circumstances. His work is in the general interest of the community and is facilitated by the co-operation of a number of other disciplines, only some of which have been mentioned here. It is particularly true in the case of sudden or unexplained death that 'justice must not only be done but must be seen to be done', and the findings at inquest may often remove suspicion or doubt of the innocent.

Co-operation between doctors and the coroner is essential and this has become so well established that the highest proportion of cases come from this source. It is quite possible that the theatre nurse will have to attend a coroner's court at some time in her career and familiarity with court procedure will do much to lessen her fears or anxiety. It is not the coroner's responsibility to proportion blame and the nurse, if called as a witness, should present her evidence in clear, simple language, avoiding medical terms if possible.

A knowledge of the procedures for dealing with particular cases, e.g. murder or infection, can only help the nurse to care for herself and her patients more intelligently and increase her awareness of the importance of liaising with other staff and agencies.

### Acknowledgements

Doctor Olga High, Chief Medical Laboratory Scientific Officer, Department of Histopathology, Guy's Hospital, London; Mr Peter Everett, Mortuary Superintendent, Her Majesty's Coroner's Court, Tennis St, London, for his invaluable help; Mr Peter Kersey, Postmortem Technician, Guy's Hospital London.

# References

1. Births and Deaths Registration Act 1874, 1926, 1953.
2. Medical Protection Society, Statutory notifications: Reporting deaths to the coroner, 1977.
3. 'Increased risk from viral hepatitis', *Nursing Standard*, 16 December 1982.
4. S. Polakoff and H.E. Tillett, 'Acute viral hepatitis B; laboratory reports 1975-1979', *British Medical Journal*, vol. 284, p. 1881, 19 June 1982.
5. Criminal Law Act 1977.
6. C.J. Polson, R.P. Brittain and T.K. Marshall, *The Disposal of the Dead*, 2nd ed., English Universities Press, 1962, ch. 3, p.43.
7. Ibid., ch. 20, p. 253.
8. S.H. Burges and J.E. Hilton (eds.), *The New Police Surgeon: A Practical Guide*, Hutchinson, 1987.

Much useful information can be gained from the following:

Peter Everett, 'The modern post-mortem room', *Nursing Mirror*, 25 August 1975.

Peter Everett, 'A case for justice', *Nursing Mirror*, 15 November 1979.

Keith Simpson, *Forensic Medicine*, 7th ed., Edward Arnold, 1979.

*The Work of a Coroner, a Home Office Guide*, HMSO, 1981.

# 12 INTERNATIONAL LEGAL POSITIONS ON SURGERY

In many areas of surgery the Law develops piecemeal in response to specific problems and the same principle applies at international level. In a world where all men are supposedly equal there are still many places where some are more equal than others. This dominion over our fellow man can be largely due to having greater power and more money; but of course this is not the whole story. Ignorance, fear, the absence of any educational or health care facilities, a sometimes fanatical adherence to religious beliefs and customs, and overwhelming poverty are just some of the handicaps of people in the underdeveloped countries.

By comparison, we in the developed countries are wealthy beyond belief. Without any great difficulty, we have come to take our affluence for granted and with every new surgical development we look to government to legislate further in sorting out any attendant legal problems. The people have ample opportunity to voice their opinions, the professional bodies debate and eventually yet another law is passed for our protection. All very civilised. No such problems exist in the poorer countries. For some of these people, their greatest concern may be wondering if they will live to see tomorrow. In Zimbabwe, approximately a third of all children die before 5 years of age from malnutrition. Children in this age group make up about 20 per cent of the population, but may account for up to 50 per cent of deaths.[1] In tropical areas, half a million people have lost their sight through river blindness, caused by a parasite worm, yet the medicine which could have saved their sight costs only 11p for each sufferer.[2]

During the past 20 years in the UK, we have become accustomed to public demonstrations asserting the rights of one group or another: ethnic minorities, pro-life groups, anti-vivisectionists, gay liberationists, the unemployed who believe that they should have the right to work, and more recently the women at Greenham Common. Not only are these demonstrations allowed, but also the participants are given police protection. Now, although not every demonstration is guaranteed to bring about success, it does at least serve to attract attention to a particular issue. No such demonstrations happen in the poorer countries. Apart from the fact that some of the people may not even be aware that they have any rights, autocratic governments may decide that resources are made available only to the rich, or used for purposes other than health care. In Tanzania in 1967, with an average income per head of £27, the public expenditure on health per head was £0.4, a 1.4 per cent proportion of the national income. In the same year in the Lebanon, when the average income was £176, public expenditure per head on health care was £1.2 – only 0.7 per cent of the national income.[3]

Nineteen eighty three was the 35th anniversary of the Declaration of Human Rights. The 31 articles of this Bill state the fundamental minimum rights of every human being. The World Health Organization continues its campaign against deadly and destructive diseases and the International Council of Nurses continues to work for the availability and accessibility of health care for all. Despite all this, one billion people in the developing countries are still without enough food to eat and many of them are dying from infectious diseases because immunisation is not available.[4] When we think about these problems, it must make us realise that here in Britain we are privileged, spoiled, cocooned and cosseted. Theatre nurses sit at procedure meetings for hours arguing as to whether the scalpel should be on the right or left of the pre-packed set of instruments. We use all the available facilities with little or no thought for the cost and extravagance is accepted as inevitable. We are so conditioned to having everything we need, available on demand, that when even one item is not forthcoming, a major crisis can develop in the health service.

We have laws, rules, policies and procedures to cover every eventuality, job descriptions which ensure that we only do certain tasks, the United Kingdom Central Council to determine nursing standards and discipline and generally ensure that professional standards are maintained. Not all nurses are so privileged. In some of the developing countries the Law, as we understand it, does not exist, and even if it did, its application would be a virtual impossibility. Attempts are being made by voluntary agencies and various mission groups to develop health services in these countries, many relying totally on funds and staff from their home country, but with the pressing immediate problems, plans can only be long-term and there continues to be a serious shortage of doctors and nurses. At least in many of these countries, nurses do not have to concern themselves with the many issues which worry us in the UK: the extended role, accountability, negligence, or the Nursing Process. They are allowed to use their skills to the full, training local people in simple basic nursing skills, giving medical aid, sometimes with the most primitive equipment, and working round the clock in an effort to cope with appalling health and social conditions. No time is wasted there discussing the implementation of a 37$\frac{1}{2}$ hour week.

There are no international laws relating to surgery. However, in the developed countries there are similarities in laws, although each country has some laws which are peculiar to that country alone. Countries within the European Economic Community are subject to the Treaty of Rome and the legislation made under its terms. The Community Court of Justice at Luxemburg is responsible for interpreting Community measures and dealing with conflicts between member states, and EEC law can now prevail over United Kingdom law.

The Treaty allows for free movement of doctors, general nurses and some other professions, across the national boundaries of member states, subject to certain conditions, e.g. qualifications based on certain academic standards, linguistic competence and a knowledge of the professional ethics of the host member state. Since implementing this agreement is obviously an enormous task, the difference in nursing law in member states, and the complete absence of a professional disciplinary system in some of the countries, can be both disturbing and confusing for the British nurse, whose standards have traditionally been so well protected by the General Nursing Council. Thus there is an obvious need within the EEC for a uniform machinery of nurse discipline to protect the public from unsafe practitioners.

Inevitably integration will be slow, and this applies much more in the health care field than in agriculture or trade policies. The National Health system in Britain has been accused of having shortcomings but there are many distinct features of it which are worth retaining, such as the availability of treatment for all and accessibility to the most advanced forms of equipment for diagnosis and treatment, e.g. lasers and body scanners. The other great advantage of the system is that patients do not have to worry about being presented with an enormous bill and they also know that as far as is possible their wishes with regard to treatment will be respected. So although the countries within the EEC encompass Belgium, Denmark, France, Germany, Greece, Eire, Italy, Luxembourg, Netherlands and the United Kingdom, it is fair to say that none of these countries has a health service comparable to Britain's.

Disease is universal, but the means available to treat it and the legal problems for doctors, nurses and patients, vary enormously. In some countries, the very need for medical attention will be determined by religion, while in other, more health-conscious, countries the people clamour daily for an increase in health care facilities, despite the fact that millions are already being spent.

I have not written a detailed account of the legal problems associated with surgery at international leve' There are so many variables affecting attitudes and governmε 'hinking on health care in individual countries, that comparisous as such would be impossible. For example, 'in Turkey in 1972, training for the university nurse was still directed by a doctor . . . the country had six doctors to one nurse . . . Student nurses themselves gave the only nursing in ward and theatre'.[5] Efforts are being made by the World Health Organization to collect health statistics but 'vital information of the simplest kind was available for only half the world's population'.[6] Therefore the information contained in this chapter is very general and is written with the hope that it will help the reader to understand the variation in health care and the different powers and interpretations of the Law in some countries.

## The United States of America

The health care industry is the second largest employer (after education) in America. Of its 7 million employees, 450,000 are doctors and 1.5 million are nurses; yet despite these great numbers there are 150 places where there are no doctors.

Nurse education in the United States is very different to Britain; in the UK the students gain their practical experience in the clinical area, with the minimum of supervision, but for students in many American hospitals the practical experience they can gain is limited because of the Patients Bill of Rights which entitles them to be cared for by trained nurses. The Nurse Practitioner is a special type of nurse in the USA. She performs many of the tasks which in the UK would be seen as the doctor's responsibility and in some rural areas she may be the primary or only health care provider.

Nurses employed in the operating room are faced with many problems, some of which seem as though they will never be resolved. These include increased concern about the growing number of surgeon's assistants and operating room technicians employed, the absence in some hospitals of any policy regarding counts, the decision of some hospital authorities to dispense with surgical consent forms, relying totally on implied consent, and the continuing and overriding authority of the surgeons in decision-making. Also, possibly because of the size of the country, there is a great variation in the Law as it applies to nursing in different states and also from one hospital to another. The Association of Operating Room Nurses works relentlessly in an attempt to establish a uniform standard for patient care in the operating room but their task is hampered by problems well known to us in Britain: lack of finance and staff and a reluctance on the part of some surgeons and nurses to accept change.

All operating room nurses must carry malpractice insurance and it is not unusual to read of individual nurses being sued in the Courts. It is said in the States that the 'captain of the ship' doctrine is dying,[7] and more and more the Courts are modifying this doctrine and apportioning blame in malpractice suits between the surgeon and the operating room nurse.

A patient sued a physician and a hospital because a haemostat was left in his abdomen during surgery. The jury's award of 315,000 dollars was charged against the Surgeon. He appealed and lost on the grounds that he was in exclusive control of the OR . . . but a higher Court reversed the decision, saying that the hospital clearly exercised a large degree of control over those matters essential to an operation . . . the damaging evidence, in the Court's opinion, was that the nurses counted instruments before packing them for an operation, but counted only swabs afterwards – according to the hospital's procedure. . .

The Court found the hospital liable for not devising adequate procedures for its operating room personnel.[7]

There is a strong resistance to the role of the midwife in the States and from the legal viewpoint she is in a precarious position. Most practise without insurance, as the premiums are extremely high. Prosecution in most cases is instigated by obstetricians and it is rumoured that this is due to the doctor's desire to monopolise this financially lucrative area of health care.[9]

Medical malpractice in the States has been continually publicised, and between 1960 and 1970, premiums for malpractice insurance rose by 949.2 per cent.[10] The criteria for standards of care are exactly the same for doctors and nurses in the States as they are in the UK, i.e. that of a 'reasonable' doctor or nurse, and this view is upheld by the Courts. The overwhelming publicity accorded medical malpractice may be partly accounted for by the very size of the country, but it could also be due to the practice of 'legal medicine'. This is a thriving business where the patient is likely to be given professional advise about possible malpractice by insurance brokers even before anything has actually gone wrong. Evidence is emerging that physicians are tending to increase the number of diagnostic tests performed and that they are 'becoming more wary of "high risk" procedures and suit-prone patients'.[11] A national poll by the American Medical Association found that about 75 per cent of the physicians polled were practising 'defensive medicine', that is ordering X-rays, laboratory work-ups and other diagnostic tests to build up a protective file. Nine out of ten doctors reported that they were significantly concerned about potential malpractice suits.[12]

## Africa

For many people in the African continent, hospitals are places where they go to die. The killing of female infants is a deep-rooted custom with nomads and hunters and the medicine-man is often preferred to the conventional doctor.

Female circumcision is a traditional practice of some groups in Africa. The three basic types are: Sunna circumcision, which is the removal of the clitoral prepuce; excision or clitoridectomy, which can include minora and part or most of the external genitalia; and infibulation, which is closing of the vagina by suturing or the use of some other type of fastening device immediately after excision (a small opening is left for urinating and menstruation). This ritual is performed to ensure fidelity and is a religious and cultural practice. The procedure is usually carried out by old women of the village and no form of anaesthetic is used.[13] The practice has now been banned in Kenya by the government.

In South Africa, the law relating to the taking of donor organs has some similarity to the law in Britain. In his book *One Life*, Christiaan Barnard describes the way in which he tackled the problem.

> Any person dying from unnatural causes . . . must legally undergo post-mortem. . . . During the post-mortem, one or another organ may legally be removed for purposes of teaching or study, provided the parents or relatives give consent. We intended to operate within the law, putting the kidney or heart within a new body, rather than in a bottle on a shelf . . . we decided that none of the doctors involved in the transplant would pronounce on the death of a potential donor. This would be done by a separate neurological team.

The legalities were cleared with Dr Lionel S. Smith, Professor of Forensic Medicine.[14]

> Pretoria: A father of ten was decapitated with a butcher's knife on the orders of a witch doctor, a court trying three blacks for murder was told.[15]


**France**

Although France does not have a complete system of health care, most of the population are covered by compulsory sickness insurance which covers treatment of all kinds. The Deontological Code (Decree of 28 November 1955) laid down the basic principles of 'liberal' medicine giving the patient the right to choose his doctor, the doctor the right to prescribe and with payment of fees by the patient to the doctor by direct negotiation. The patient then recoups his expenses from his insurance office. Since 1971, there has been a national agreement which fixes the rate for various forms of treatment. There has been considerable expansion in training of paramedical staff in the last 20 years, but there continues to be a shortage of applicants for nurse training, possibly because of the poor image and low wage of nurses.[16]

The Caillavet Law, introduced in 1976, allows for the removal of organs for scientific or therapeutic purposes, immediately after death, unless the deceased has specifically stated an objection in life.[17]

**Soviet Union**

Preventive medicine is the fundamental principle behind Soviet health care and the state guarantees material security for the sick, the elderly and those in need. There are 30,000 polyclinics (1975) in the USSR providing preventive and curative treatment and patients may be referred from the polyclinics to a hospital. Health programmes are developed with the support and participation of the people and all medical treatment is free.[18]

Nurse anaesthetists, supervised by a medical anaesthetist, are employed, two responsible for each patient, but three during open-heart surgery. I cannot comment on all the practices in Soviet operating theatres, but it is not routine practice to count swabs and instruments.

Kidney transplantation is a popular operation and the legal rulings for removal or donation of organs are the same as in Britain. Nurses are not held legally responsible for their actions; they are at all times responsible to the doctor, who in turn is responsible for their actions and for the patient.[19]

**Italy**

Italians have a compulsory health care insurance but there continues to be a marked inequality between the services available for the affluent and those for the very poor, of which there are many, particularly in southern Italy. The single largest group of staff associated with nursing are nurses' aids (60,000 in 1975), and their training lasts for one year. The training period to qualify as a nurse is two years but there continues to be an acute shortage of nurses. In 1975, there were 35,000 trained nurses and efforts are being made to increase this number. Private medical care continues to be a lucrative business. In 1981 a number of doctors were arrested for 'selling' state hospital beds to patients who wanted immediate treatment. In Court a patient stated that a doctor asked her for 250,000 lire to admit her son to a hospital. The Italians called the scandal 'the golden beds case'.[20]

## Middle Eastern Countries

Most countries in this area are run on strict Muslim rules, and these dictate the behaviour of the people and the Law. Serious offences are tried in a religious court and defence is negligible. There are basically three parts to the law: homicide and wounding are treated as civil wrongs which result in blood-money or compensation for the injured party; very severe penalties are imposed for a few serious crimes, e.g. illicit sex relations, theft, consumption of alcohol and brigandage; the death penalty is imposed for the abandonment of the Islamic faith, for murder and for adultery. In 1981, cases were reliably reported in a Middle East country of four surgeons who left swabs in abdominal cavities during surgery. In each case the theatre nurses were held primarily responsible for the incidents. They were each fined one month's salary and expelled from the country. The surgeons were fined seven days' salary and harshly reproached.

## Egypt

For all practical purposes legal considerations are non-existent here, but various nursing organisations are endeavouring to introduce the concept of legal rights. Malpractice suits are rare and the doctor's role is generally considered as being above reproach. Professional nursing as such is non-existent and the staff who assist at surgery are no more than aides.[21]

## Israel

The traditional homeland of the Jewish people has a long tradition of care of the sick, based on biblical and Talmudic beliefs. Hospital services are provided mainly by the Ministry of Health and voluntary health insurance (*Kupat Holim*) covers over 90 per cent of the population for medical care. There are 19 schools of nursing in the country, some now offering accredited courses in association with a university and all basing their training programmes very much on the American system. The emergence of the new highly-qualified nurse has caused some conflict in the established nurse-doctor relationship, which in the past limited the nurse's authority.

Abortion for healthy married women is only available on a private, unofficial basis and the decision to terminate any pregnancy is made by a professional committee in which nurses are not included. This is a contentious issue for nurses, particularly when a midtrimester termination is performed. They maintain that they should have a voice in the decision, as they are intimately involved in the procedure, caring for the patient in labour and the delivery of the dead foetus.[22]

Informed consent is normally a prerequisite for surgery, but relatives' permission is not required to remove a donor organ from a dead body.[23]

## Australia

Australia operates schemes of medical care, financed by the state or by insurance, according to taste.[24] The standard of care required of a doctor or nurse is exactly the same as in the UK, and although British influence has declined in Australia, Court decisions in cases of malpractice continue to be influenced by decisions made in the English Courts. The following case in which the patient sued two medical practitioners, a surgeon and an anaesthetist, for negligence whilst performing an operation upon her whereby she was seriously burned and otherwise 'injured', helps to illustrate the responsibility of the theatre nursing staff in providing a safe environment in the operating theatre.

The surgeon was operating to remove a kidney; the theatre

was heated by an electric fire consisting of elements which became red hot when switched on; the anaesthetist was using ether; someone dropped the bottle, the fumes went on to the fire, caught fire and burned the patient's hand. The Court findings were that the doctors were entitled to assume – in the absence of notice to the contrary – that the theatre was in a suitable condition to enable them to carry out their work, and generally that the preparations were such that all they would have to do would be to concentrate on the performance of their respective parts of the operation. It was therefore the judge's view that the doctors could only be liable for negligence if there was evidence that they knew the type of heating which was being used, and also if they knew that the theatre sister had failed in her duty to switch it off.[25] Surely a timely warning here for us all.

## New Zealand

The law in New Zealand is founded on the Common Law of England and criminal law has particular relevance to medical practice. The crimes Act (NZ) 1961, Section 155, states

> everyone who undertakes (except in case of necessity) to administer surgical or medical treatment, or to do any other lawful act the doing of which is or may be dangerous to life, is under a legal duty to have and to use reasonable knowledge, skill and care in doing any such act, and is criminally responsible for the consequences of omitting without lawful excuse to discharge that duty.

The rulings with regard to consent to treatment are similar to those in the UK. The Contraception, Sterilisation and Abortion Act 1977 (and amendments), allow for the legal termination of pregnancy, subject to the conditions of the Act, which also has a 'conscience' clause in the final section, making it clear that

> doctors and nurses are not under any obligation to: perform or assist in the performance of an abortion, or any operations for the purpose of rendering the patient sterile or for fitting, supplying to administer, or assisting in the supply or administering of any contraceptives, or to offer or give any advice relating to contraception.

The Accident Compensation Act 1972 (and further parts and amendments), makes provision for safety and the prevention of accidents; for the rehabilitation and compensation of persons who suffer personal injury by accident in respect of which they have cover under this Act; for the compensation of certain dependants of those persons where death results from the injury; and for the 'abolition as far as practicable of actions for damages arising directly or indirectly out of personal injury by accident and death resulting therefrom and certain other actions'. In essence, this Act provides a 'no fault' compensation for those who suffer as the result of an accident and if an event is accepted as an accident under the Act, then a patient cannot sue.

**Summary**

The purpose of any health service should be to provide, as effectively as possible, a medical and often medico-social solution to the problems of its users. Despite the remarkable progress which has been made worldwide, we are still a long way from providing this, as a right, for every human being. For the millions of people who are still deprived of this right, the availability of even basic human needs will continue to be of greater importance than any legal sanctions. Fear and suspicion of medical science, which may be seen as an effort to replace religions, can prevent some people from accepting much needed help.

As the power of the doctor diminishes in the Western world, so the power of the lawyer will increase. We may look to the USA now as 'the land of malpractice', but increased awareness of rights and press coverage of medical misdemeanours can only serve to increase the public's demands for international laws to protect them when they are ill.

Most 'civilised' countries afford some legal protection for patients, doctors and nurses, but there are still many areas of the world where even basic human rights are denied.

**References and Note**

1. Graham Anderson, 'Birth of a Health Service', *Nursing Times*, 27 April 1983.
2. Andrea Kon, 'Don't let another child go blind', *News of the World Magazine*, 19 June 1983.

3. Fourth Report of the World Health Situation 1965-8, WHO, Geneva, 1971.
4. Patricia Patterson, "'Health for all" is nurse's goal for world's people', *AORN Journal*, vol. 34, no. 3, September 1981, pp. 450-1.
5. Fraser Brockington, 'A permanent framework for general Public Health for underdeveloped countries', in *World Health*, 3rd ed., Churchill Livingstone, 1975, p. 203.
6. 'Some important health statistics available in various countries', bulletin of the WHO 11, pp. 201-8.
7. The 'Captain of the ship' doctrine was, until recent years, a guiding legal precept in the States. The surgeon was held to be responsible for everything that went on in the operating room. The theory was that the patient chose the surgeon and he was therefore responsible for the surgical procedure and also for the staff assisting. It is gradually being recognised by the American courts that all professionals involved in a surgical procedure bear moral and legal responsibility for their actions.
8. Jack L. Mumme, *Seven Surefire Ways to Lose a Malpractice Case*, Downey, California, November 1977, p. 61.
9. Kate Newson, 'Outlaws in the west', *Nursing Mirror*, 18 August 1982.
10. HEW Report of the Secretary's Commission on Medical Malpractice, 1973.
11. *American Medical News*, 7 March 1977.
12. *American Medical News*, 4 April 1977.
13. 'Female circumcision, excision and infibulation: the facts and proposals for change', Minority Rights Group, Report No. 47.
14. Christiaan Barnard and Bill Curtis Pepper, *One Life*, Harrap, 1969.
15. *Evening Standard*, 18 May 1983.
16. Tony Smith, 'I left my heart . . .', *The Times Health Supplement*, 20 November 1981.
17. Alan Maynard, *Health Care in the European Community*, Croom Helm, 1975, pp. 137-8.
18. Fraser Brockington, 'The creation of a Public Health structure', in *World Health*.
19. M. Millington, 'Study tour of hospitals and polyclinics in the USSR', *National Association of Theatre Nurses Journal*, 18 September 1977.
20. John Phillips, 'Doctors go feather bedding', *The Times Health Supplement*, 20 November 1981.
21. Margaret Nyssen, 'Legal considerations for safe practice in the operating room (Cairo, Egypt)', Second World Congress of Operating Room Nurses, Lausanne, August 1981.
22. Shoshana Abbudi, 'Midtrimester termination of pregnancy', First International Congress of Nursing Law and Ethics, Jerusalem, June 1982.
23. R.Y. Calne, 'Ethics, the Law and the future', in *Clinical Organ Transplantation*, Blackwell Scientific Publications, 1971, p. 522.
24. Fraser Brockington, 'The European movement', in *World Health*.
25. Leahy J. Taylor, *Medical Malpractice*, John Wright & Sons, 1980. Ch. 8, Medical malpractice in Australia, p. 203, Paton v. Parker.

# TABLE OF STATUTES AND STATUTORY INSTRUMENTS USED FOR REFERENCE

Abortion Act 1967, and Abortion Regulations 1968
Accident Compensation Act 1972 (New Zealand)
Anatomy Act 1832, and minor amendment 1871
Births and Deaths Registration Act 1953
Caillavet Law 1976 (France)
Coroner's Act 1887, and Coroner's Amendment Act 1926
Cremation Act 1902
Contraception, Sterilisation and Abortion Act 1977 (New Zealand)
Crimes Act 1961 (New Zealand)
Criminal Law Act 1977
Data Protection Bill 1982
Employers Liability (Compulsory Insurance) Act 1969
Employment Protection Act 1975
Equal Pay Act 1970
Family Law Reform Act 1969
Fatal Accidents Inquiry (Scotland) Act 1895
Fatal Accidents and Sudden Deaths Inquiry (Scotland) Act 1906
Fire Precautions Act 1971
Health and Safety at Work Act 1974
Human Tissue Act 1961, and Human Tissue Act (Northern Ireland) 1962
Infant Life (Preservation) Act 1929
Medicines Act 1968
Mental Health Act 1959, and Mental Health (Amendment) Act 1982
National Health Service Act 1977
Perjury Act 1911
Police and Criminal Evidence Bill 1982
Rehabilitation of Offenders Act 1974
Sex Discrimination Act 1975
Treaty of Union 1707
Wills Act 1837 and 1968

## Reports

Howie Report 1978
Lewin Report 1970
Salmon Report 1966

Copies of statutes/statutory instruments and reports relating to the British Isles are available from Her Majesty's Stationery Office, London

# INDEX

abbreviations, use of 50-1
abortion: on demand 10
	husband's attempt to prevent 14
Abortion Act 1967 14, 43
Adventists 34
Africa 129-30
anaesthetic accidents 17, 66-8, 112
anaesthetic room, accidents in 66-8
anaesthetist: duty *re* drugs 66, 112
	explanation to patient 44
Anatomy Act 1832 117-18
Arthur, Dr L. 85
artificial insemination 103-4
	donor 103-4
	husband 103
	religious attitudes 106
	sperm bank 104
artificial reproduction 103-6
American Indians 34
Armenians 34
artificial vagina fashioning, wife's
	objection to 43
Assembly of God Foursquare Church
	(Pentecostals) 37
Australia 133-4

'baby bank' 98
'baby farm' 98, 99
Baha'i 34
Baptists 34
Barnaard, Christian 95
	quoted 130
Blankfield, Mrs Harriet 99
bone marrow transplant 103
brain death 90-1
Brown, Carol 19
Brysson-Whyte, Miss, quoted 54
Buddhists 34-5

Christian Scientists 33-4
Church of Jesus Christ of Latter-day
	Saints (Mormons) 37
communicable disease 114
communication: lack of 49-55
	in operating theatre 50-1
		barriers to 49
		non-verbal 53

computers 81
confidentiality 76-7
congenital abnormality, child with 41,
	79
Congenital Disabilities (Civil Liability)
	Act 1976 79
consent to examination not required 24
consent to surgery 22-9
	age of 24-5
	children 25
	definition 22
	emergency situation 28-9
	forms 26-7
	informed consent: who can give 23
		who cannot give 23-4
	types: implied 25
		oral 25
		written 25-8
	USA 27
controlled drugs in theatre 67
corneal transplant 102
coroner 109-10
	deaths reported to 110-11
coroner's court 109-23
cot death 115
counsellor 28
Cremation Act 1902 121
Crown Court 116-17

Data Protection Bill 81
death: accidents and injuries contri-
		buting to 112
	ill-treatment as cause 113-14
	sudden 111
Declaration of Human Rights 125
diathermy accident 57
Dickens, Charles 10
disclosure of information 76-7
doctor: records 75
	responsibilities 19-20
Down, Mary, quoted 17
Down's baby cases 86
drugs: anaesthetist's duty 66, 112
	in operating theatre 67, 113
Duncan, Carlton & Sati 98-9
dying patient 83-92

economy 71-2
egg grafts 104-5
electrosurgery 69-70
Employers Liability (Compulsory
    Insurance) Act 1969 71
Employment Protection Act 1975 10
Equal Pay Act 1970 10, 40
equipment, modern 64
Ethical Committee, hospital 45
European Economic Community
    (EEC) 49-50, 126
euthanasia 10, 88-90

Family Law Reform Act 1969 102
female circumcision 46, 129-30
fertilisation *in vitro* 14, 98, 105
Finsberg, Geoffrey, quoted 97
fire 69
Fire Precautions Act 1971 69
France 130-1
Fowler, Norman, quoted 61
freedom, personal 9-10
Friends (Quakers) 37

General Nursing Council 10
    disciplinary action 60
    EEC nursing directives 49-50
    on strike/industrial action by nurses
        13
*General Textbook of Nursing* (E.
    Pearce) 84
Greek Orthodox 36-7
Greene, Harry, quoted 7
Grey, Professor Peter 42
*Guidelines on Confidentiality in
    Nursing* (Royal College of Nursing)
    76-7

Health and Safety at Work Act 1974
    69, 70, 111, 114
Health Authority, liability to pay
    damages 71
Health Visitor, alleged misconduct 60
heart transplant 102
hemimandibulectomy, patient after 85
Hindus 35
hospitals, closure of 97
Howie Report 1978 119-20
Human Tissue Act 1961 101, 117
Human Tissue Act (Northern Ireland)
    1962 101
Humphry, Jean 89
husband's male organs, wife's
    objection to removal of 43

hysterectomy 40

ill-treatment 113-14
industrial disease 114
Industrial Relations Act 1971 76
infant deaths 115
Infant Life (Preservation) Act 1929 43
information: disclosure, regarding staff
    79
    giving to patients and relatives 78-9
    giving to press 78
inquest 115-16
instruments, retained 57-8
insurance, indemnity 57
International Council of Nurses 9
Israel 133
Italy 131-2

Jehovah's Witnesses 32-3
    blood refused 39
    charged with homicide 39
Jews 38
Joint Board of Clinical Nursing
    Studies, theatre courses 63

Kent and Canterbury Hospital,
    anaesthetic accident 17

lasers 68
last offices, danger of infection 119-20
law 9
    English 7, 9
        case law 9
        statute law 9
Lewin Report (HMSO, 1968) 20
Light, Claire 42
Limitation Act 1975 79

Married Women's Property Act 1882
    39, 40
Medical Defence Union, on termina-
    tion of pregnancy on child 43
Medicines Act 1968 67
Mental Health Act 1959 23, 43
Mental Health (Amendment) Act
    1982: consent to treatment 24, 43-4
    patient's objection to treatment 43-
        4
    second opinion on surgical
        operation on brain 24
Mental Health (Scotland) Act 1960 43
Metropolitan Poor Law Act 1867 11
Middle Eastern countries 132
Mormons (Church of Jesus Christ of

# Index

Latter-day Saints) 37
Muslims 35-6

National Health Service, staff cuts 61
National Health Service Act 1977 11-12
negligence: definition 56
    in operating theatre 60-1
    nurse's liability 56-62
New Zealand 134-5
Nightingale, Florence 16
nurse 10
    accompanying patient to theatre 65-6
    anaesthetised patient 18
    communication with other nurses 49-50
    from other EEC countries 50
    incapacity 60
    intensive care unit 18
    liability for negligence 56-62
    member of multidisciplinary team 18
    'mini-surgeon' 16
    objectives in training/education 56
    professional misconduct 13
    reasonable 56
    records of 76
    records made by 75
    see also theatre nurse
Nurse Manager 68
Nursing Process 63

objections by patients to be used for teaching/research 44-5
objections to surgery 30-48
    by parent/guardian 41-2
    by spouse 39-41
    parent's, to termination of pregnancy on child 43
    religious 31-9
    who can object 30
    who cannot object 30-1
    wife's, to removal of husband's male organs/fashioning of artificial vagina 43
objections to treatment by mentally ill/handicapped patients 43-4
Operating Department Assistant (ODA) 20, 68
operating theatre: accidents in 63
    communication in 50-1
    barriers to 49
    non-verbal 53

ethical decision making in 85
negligence in 60-1
records 75
operation register 74
organ transplantation 94-108
    bone marrow 103
    cornea 102-3
    heart 102
    legal problems 100-1
    live related donor 101-2
    moral problems 106

Pankhurst, Christabel 40
Pankhurst, Emmeline 39-40
patient: accidents to 64-70
    arrival in theatre 66-7
    giving information to 78
    identification in theatre 51-2, 66
    on way to theatre 65-6
    post-operative, untrained nurse in charge 17
    records 75-6
    wrong one sent to theatre 65
Pentecostals (Assembly of God Foursquare Church) 37
Perjury Act 1911 110
picketing 12
plastic surgeon, breach of contract 28
Police and Criminal Evidence Bill 74, 80
Poor Law 11
post-mortem examination 117-18
press, giving of information to 78
preventive medicine 97

Quakers (Friends) 37

record, definition 82
records: keeping 73-82
    retention time limits 79-80
Register of Nurses, Scotland 10
Rehabilitation of Offenders Act 1974 75, 79
relatives, giving information to 78
report 73-4
    definition 73
retained foreign bodies 57-9
right to life 10
Ritchie, George 90-1
Roman Catholics 37
Ross, Donald 95
Royal College of Nursing: Rule 12 13
    terminal care forum 84
Russian Orthodox 38

Rye, David, quoted 86

'Safeguards against Wrong Operations'
   (Medical Defence Union, Royal
   College of Nursing, 1978) 50-1,
   51-2
safety signs in workplace 53
Scotland, legal proceedings in 121-2
*Second Life* (S. Cook, 1982) 32
Sex Discrimination Act 1975  10, 40
sharps disposal 70
Sikhs 36
Soviet Union 131
specimen labelling 51
*Speller's Law Relating to Hospitals and
   Kindred Institutions* (J. Jacob,
   1978), 29
   forms of consent 43
sperm bank 104
staff: disclosure of information about
   79
   protection 71
Statutory Instrument 1980 No. 1471
   (Health and Safety Commission)
   53
stillbirth 115
stoma therapist 28
surrogate mothers (womb-leasing)
   105-6
swabs: cutting of radio-opaque 59
   retained 57-9

terminal, definition 83

terminal illness 83-92
termination, definition 83
termination of pregnancy on child,
   parent's objection 43
test-tube baby 14, 105
theatre nurse 16
   duties 16
   professional behaviour 11
   role 18-20
Trade Union and Labour Relations
   Act 1974  12
Treaty of Rome 126
trolley 65
Turkish towels 58

United Kingdom Central Council,
   disciplinary case 60
United States of America 18, 127-9

Victoria Hospital, Workshop 17
viral hepatitis 114

Weinrich, Heidi, quoted 50
Westminster Hospital, anaesthetic
   accident 17
womb-leasing (surrogate mothers)
   105-6
women, granting of vote to 40
Women's Franchise League 39
Wrack, Peter, quoted 42
wrong operations 59-61

Yates, Alan 95